About the Author

The author has been running regularly f ... track and cross-country international in the ... ' in the Kentmere Horsehoe, Fairfield H ... and set a record for the Carnethy Hil ... ays, and participates in parkruns from time t

Alistair Blamire was director of an ... in Edinburgh from 1981 until his retirement in 2016.

Also by Alistair Blamire:

The Green Machine:

The Story of Edinburgh University Hare and Hounds 1960-1970

'Young athletes nowadays will learn a lot about how to improve their running; older, nostalgic readers will appreciate insider anecdotes and Alistair Blamire's crystal-clear perspective on an important era in Scottish Athletics'

Colin Youngson (in Scottish Distance Running History, November 2017)

'UK track international athlete Alistair Blamire has written a most engaging book covering the most successful period of the Edinburgh University Hare and Hounds, a long-established university cross country club in which he was an active member in the 1960s and early 1970s'

Ian Tempest (in 'Track Stats', the Quarterly Bulletin of the National Union of Track Statisticians, May 2018)

'This profusely illustrated 131 page publication also includes a well-researched, concise history of middle and long distance training methods, citing such influential figures as Woldemar Gerschler, Franz Stampfl, Percy Cerutty and Arthur Lydiard'

Mel Watman, Former Editor of Athletics Weekly (in Athletics International, July 2018)

JOGGING TRAILS IN SOUTH LAKELAND

A Guide to Rural Running

Alistair Blamire

Printed by

Crawford Print and Design Ltd
25 Rodney Street, Edinburgh, EH7 4EL
Tel: 0131 558 9755 Email: susan@crawfordprint.co.uk
www.crawfordprint.co.uk

Published by ELS Press, 2021

ISBN 978-1-5272-9461-5

FOR POLLY, WHO GAVE RUNNING A TRY

CONTENTS

PREFACE

This book has evolved over several years. It's a combination of two great passions of mine - the challenges and sense of achievement offered by long distance running, and the unique landscape of South Lakeland – which I hope will inspire others to share and enjoy.

My family has a long association with the Lake District. My paternal grandfather came from the village of Staveley near Kendal where his father had been the manager of Martin's Bank, and the postmaster, in the late 19th and early 20th centuries. My grandfather went to St Hild and St Bede College in Durham where he studied to become a schoolteacher and his first post was in Edinburgh. In Edinburgh, he met my grandmother, married and raised a family and lived there for the rest of his life. In due course he became headmaster of both Colinton and London Street Primary Schools. After he retired from teaching, he was ordained in the Scottish Episcopal Church, serving as curate at St Cuthbert's Episcopal Church in Colinton and as Episcopal priest for the Dreghorn Army Barracks.

As a result of these connections our (mostly Edinburgh) family rented a cottage at the aptly named settlement of lead miners' cottages at Seldomseen in Glencoyne, near Ullswater, from the early 1930s. Then from 1939 they moved to more familiar territory, taking over the lease of a small cottage on High House farm, on the fells between Windermere and Staveley. We spent many holidays there from that time, in the basic circumstances (there was no bath or running hot water or water closet) which were common for the immediate post-war period. Before long we developed, primarily through my father who was a relentless walker, often on his own, a love of the fells and the many walks in the area which could be accessed directly from the cottage door.

In the meantime, my own preoccupation for long distance running developed from primary school days, inspired by the great British distance runners of the time, and the epic battles on the track between Landy and Bannister, and Kuts and Pirie and, later on, the emergence of Herb Elliott and Peter Snell. My siblings and I, and our invited friends, egged on by me, would attempt to replicate the achievements of our heroes, indulging in races to the neighbouring farm and back or down the farm access track to the main road, often in pursuit of the farm tractor as it headed off to deliver milk for neighbouring communities.

Most of our walking sorties were on trails near the cottage and more often than not on the fell tops of Ill Bell and Sallows and Sour Howes. In the early days we didn't have a car, so the idea of wandering further than this direct area rarely occurred to us. When the car came along, we ventured into the Central Lakes and the goal was always one of reaching tops such as Helvellyn, Scafell and the Langdale Pikes, following the precise instructions of Alfred Wainwright whose exhaustive guide books were originally published from the mid-1950s. Walks on trails or at lower levels were confined to what Wainwright once described (in reference to Catbells) as 'a gentle stroll on a fine evening after a big meal'[1].

As my interest in running developed these holidays were a great opportunity to indulge in runs on the fells, accessed from the trails in the area. The runs at the time of High House coincided with my competitive running career, so I never thought about doing something too 'easy'. It was all about fell tops and I flirted briefly with fell racing in the mid-1970s, competing in the Kentmere Horseshoe race, the Fairfield Horseshoe and the Three Peaks in North Yorkshire.

In 1984 my father (the postmaster's elder grandson) 'came home' when, in his retirement, he bought a house in Staveley which had the added attractions of a flushing toilet, heating and hot water and, not least, access to shops and pubs. Staveley was well served then and has developed its commercial base hugely since, with a variety of outlets worthy of a much larger community. This was around the period when my own interest in training hard and competing seriously in cross country and track running, and the occasional fell race, began to decline. However, I moved on to a new phase of running – that of pure enjoyment, free of the pressures of serious competition and at a greatly reduced and, perhaps, more healthy level, although I have continued to compete with myself (and a few others of my vintage....) right up to the present day.

I began to investigate the trails around Staveley where I could set out for anything from 20 minutes to an hour or more and enjoy the countryside in a huge variety of options, either directly accessible from the village or, through short car runs, on roads, trails, fells or farm tracks throughout the area. In particular, Staveley opened up the possibility of discovering the intricate rights of way in the South Lakes, many of which I have detailed in this book. And it was only a matter of time before I bought my own home there in 2007.

The family's return to Staveley also coincided with the early days of the 'Jogging Boom' which had developed in the West Coast of America (particularly in Oregon), allegedly inspired by Frank Shorter's victory in the 1972 Olympic Marathon, and soon headed east to Europe. Even President Jimmy Carter went out running. Now, many more people would go out running or jogging for the purposes of health and well-being as much as for competition, and this trend has continued to develop right up to the present day.

This is a book aimed at these runners and joggers and it is not intended to be a training manual for serious athletics. Rather it's a guide to the diversity of the trails in the South Lakes area which I hope others will discover, to see them as a breath of fresh air after urban running, to revel in their variety and challenges and to enjoy the scenery and wild life. It carries the hope that others will be able to savour this activity as much as I have, whether aiming for a serious competitive level or just running for 'fun' or fitness or health or competition to whatever degree individuals wish to aspire.

AB

Staveley
April 2021

[1] In 'A Pictorial Guide to the Lakeland Fells:
Book Six – The North Western Fells', Westmorland Gazette, 1964

INTRODUCTION

A running guide isn't the same as a walking guide.

Maps or guidebooks may be part of the pleasure of a leisurely walk, but you shouldn't constantly be referring to them when you are running. For fitness as much as anything, you should run as continuously as you can when out on a trail. However, being too strict about this maxim shouldn't prevent you from enjoying interesting and varied runs, whatever the number of gates and other obstacles, and obscure changes in direction, you may encounter.

So, if you have the time, there's much to be said for walking or jog/walking the more convoluted - and perhaps more interesting - trails in advance. Take a light backpack to carry a map, and memorise the routes as much as possible in anticipation of your next visit to the area.

The trails described will give you a background in fell or trail running which you can either enjoy for its own sake or use as part of a planned training programme if you have competition in mind. They can be just as appropriate for committed fell or trail runners as they are for less serious joggers who are 'running for fun', subject to the distances travelled and the effort put into the run. But, whatever your motivation, they will help you enjoy running in the countryside, away from concerns with times and speed, from traffic, crowded places and urban environments.

If you're a serious competitive fell runner you may find that the runs seem too easy, unless you regard them as a top-up to your normal training, providing a few extra miles before a well-earned pint or supper in a nearby inn. On the other hand, if you prefer to do longer runs, once you get a feel for the huge range of options in the area, you'll be able to add to your knowledge and plan routes of your own which suit the level you are aspiring to achieve. Several of the trails described here can be combined into longer runs from the same starting point.

For joggers, to whom these trails are more specifically targeted, the short runs of 5 to 10 kilometres give a basic introduction to an activity which has huge benefits for your physical and mental well-being. But be warned: you may also be drawn into competition if the 'bug' gets you. Therefore I have included advice on how to prepare for competition, particularly if you are new to the sport.

Running can become an obsession for a number of reasons: for the physical activity itself, for the competitive element, through 'switching off' and enjoying the great outdoors for its own sake, or perhaps through a combination of all of these aspects. But whatever your motivation, it's good for you.

THE SOUTH LAKES

The designated area of South Lakeland incorporates the bustling tourist towns and villages of Windermere, Bowness, Ambleside and Grasmere. However, as you travel south east from Windermere on the main A591 road, leaving the 'chocolate box' beauty of Central Lakeland behind, you enter an altogether different landscape of rolling fields, meandering becks and grassy hillocks, stretching all the way down to the sea at Arnside and, further south, to the great expanse of Morecambe Bay. With the exception of the Kentmere and Longsleddale valleys (Wainwright's 'Far Eastern Fells') to the north of Staveley, and Dunnerdale, on the western fringe of the district, there is little in the way of mountaineering in this peaceful area of arable farms and fields of sheep and cattle, and no lakes at all.

The up and down nature of the terrain makes it especially tough for the proliferation of cyclists on the winding local roads, but an ideal environment for mountain bikers on the designated upland trails in the area, most notably around Staveley which is home to Wheelbase, one of the largest cycling outlets in the UK. But what is especially interesting for runners and joggers is the plethora of rights of way, public footpaths and bridleways which criss-cross the landscape in a complex pattern of interesting possibilities.

For some strange reason this area has never really hit it off as a venue for fell or trail running until relatively recently. Despite the huge mass participation in road and fell running which has built up over the past 40 years or so, the South Lakes can be a comparatively benign landscape for runners. But it is a potential haven for the less serious joggers who enjoy runs of up to an hour over farm tracks and fields and moorland paths.

South Lakes District Council was created when the ancient counties of Cumberland and Westmoreland were combined to form the county of Cumbria in 1974, under the Local Government Act of 1972. South Lakes covers much of the original area of Westmoreland to the south of the redesignated county, with North Lonsdale in Lancashire and the very north western corner of the Yorkshire Dales thrown in. The administrative centre is the 'auld grey town' of Kendal on the southern edge of Cumbria, which is just outside the Lake District National Park.

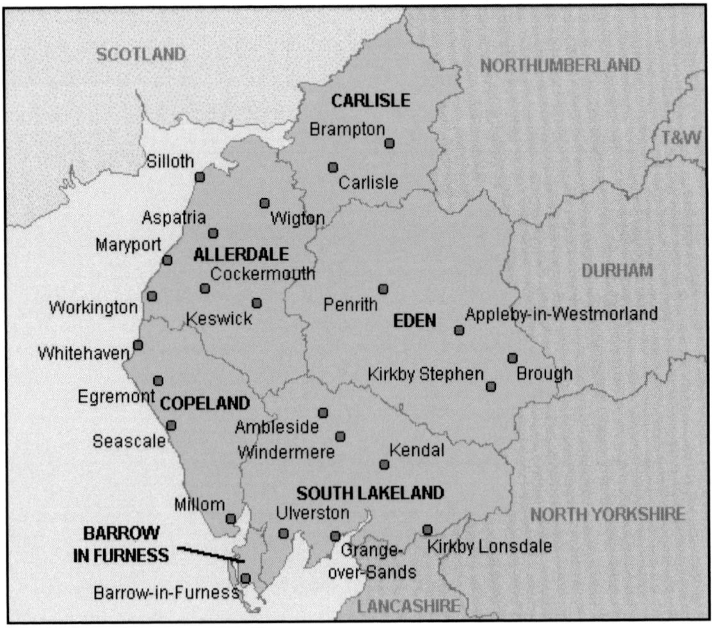

THE LOCAL COUNCILS OF CUMBRIA

The area as a whole is diverse in its characteristics, from the sparsely populated sheep farming areas of the east, far west and south, to the coastal villages of the south west – Arnside, Grange and Flookburgh – and the nearby market towns of Broughton-in-Furness and Ulverston. Tourism abounds around Lake Windermere to the north and, to a lesser extent, Lake Coniston in the near west but the southerly part of the area is much less affected by the tourism industry that consumes the more central settlements. You can often go running or walking on the fells and trails of Kentmere or Longsleddale, or Dunnerdale, and barely see anyone at all.

Almost all of the trails in this guide make use of public footpaths which allow access by foot only, and bridleways which allow access by foot, bicycle or on horseback. Motor vehicles are prohibited, with the exception of vehicles used by farmers on their own land, for example the four wheeled bikes now commonly utilised for herding sheep. Mountain biking is restricted to certain routes and, although this is difficult to oversee, it would be inadvisable for cyclists to set out on unknown and potentially inaccessible routes in any case. There are numerous recommended mountain biking trails in the South Lakes area.

The origins of public footpaths and bridleways relate to the right to travel between one place and another. Many public rights of way were created in the eighteenth and nineteenth centuries when appointed commissioners, with powers bestowed under Private Inclosure Acts, divided up and apportioned out manorial land, creating at the same time, new legal rights to cross open land. Much of this remains legally binding right up to the present day. However, there are other paths which do not appear on the register of rights of way (or Definitive Maps) created in 1947 and many historic rights of way may no longer be valid.

Legislation has been passed recently to set a deadline for clarifying the situation by January 2026 and counties like Cumbria have embarked on projects to restore and register historic public rights of way within the period imposed. In the Lake District as a whole, and the South Lakes in particular, the abundance of clear signage, both in terms of specifically directed timber signposts or coloured way markers, make it relatively easy, with just a little intuition, to follow routes on Ordnance Survey or Harveys maps.

It's important, too, to be aware of the Countryside Code[2], respecting the local people and farming communities, and protecting the natural environment. Care should be taken, for example, to ensure that gates are properly closed and don't assume that the last person through will do this if you are in a group. Be courteous when public footpaths take you along farm tracks and through farmyards and don't be inquisitive unless someone wishes to engage you.

You will often encounter fields of animals on your runs. Sheep are harmless and must not be disturbed. However, occasionally they may approach you en masse, especially in winter, thinking that you are there to feed them. Cattle are really only an issue in summer, as they are mostly kept indoors in the winter. They are also generally harmless but be more wary, don't go between a cow and its calf, and stick to field boundaries if you are uncertain.

---

[2] **The Countryside Code** is a set of guidelines for visitors to rural, and especially agricultural, regions of the United Kingdom. In 2004 it replaced The Country Code which dates back to the 1930s.

FELL RUNNING IN LAKELAND

Since the early tourism which began to develop in the late 18th and early 19th centuries through the area's close connections with writers such as Coleridge, Ruskin and Wordsworth, the Lake District has been best known for fell walking and climbing. This developed hugely with the advent of public transport and the emergence of the motor car, to the level of mass participation that we know today. However, fell running has also been extremely popular in the area, including the Yorkshire Dales and other parts of northern England, for many years.

Fell running competition originated as a professional discipline often connected to a local show or sports meeting and featured short, steep, 'up-and-down' courses which spectators could follow from the showground. The events were referred to as 'Guides Races', allegedly alluding to the fact that the competitors in the early days were almost exclusively the local men who guided hiking tourists onto the nearby fells and mountains. The first formal race of this kind took place at Grasmere in the middle of the nineteenth century and Grasmere Sports is still held in August every year. Ambleside Sports, which takes place in July, and several other pioneering events, such as the Wasdale Show and Burnsall Feast Sports, also continue to attract large fields of competitors for their fell races, right up to the present day. A second code of amateur races also developed in the mid 1800s, with the Hallam Chase in the Rivelin Valley, near Sheffield, recorded as the first amateur fell race in 1863.

Great figures from the early days of fell racing included Ernest Dalzell of Keswick, renowned for his legendary descent at Burnsall in 1910, and later, Bill Teasdale of Caldbeck, Fred Reeves of Barrow and Tommy Sedgwick of New Hutton, near Kendal. In 1977 Reeves eventually lowered Dalzell's record of 12.59 for the Burnsall race, with a time of 12.48, which still stands today[3]. These were all local professional runners, reflecting the regional nature of the sport, which has developed hugely to encompass other parts of the country in more recent times.

As fell running became more formalised the Fell Runners Association (FRA) was constituted in April 1970 with an annual championship competed for. However, the free-spirited nature of fell running and its separate amateur and professional events led to difficulties being encountered when this branch of the wider sport of athletics became more structured. Its uniqueness resulted in a dogged resistance to the machinations of the Amateur Athletics Association (AAA), based in London, which was responsible for the sport as a whole in the United Kingdom.

To add to the mix the differences between amateur and professional competition were subject at that time to the strict rules on amateurism which had existed in athletics, and in other sports such as cricket and rugby, since Victorian times. This resulted in athletes with the slightest background of having been paid to compete in any sport, being ostracised by the governing body and banned from international amateur athletics and, in particular, the Olympic Games.

It was, however, possible to be reinstated as an amateur to compete in domestic events, and the situation was further eased when the sport as a whole became 'open' in the 1980s. The AAA subsequently recognised the uniqueness of fell running and 'subcontracted' its administration to the FRA. With the advent of the 'open' era, British Athletics took on the role of the AAA from 1999. Separate bodies are also responsible for administering fell (or mountain) running in Scotland, Wales and Northern Ireland.

The first British Fell Running Championships, then known as Fell Runner of the Year, were held in 1972 with the scoring based on results in all fell races. However, in 1976 the disparity in courses was recognised and races were categorised by the amount of ascent and distance, with the most challenging being Category A[4]. At the same time the scoring was changed to allow only for each runner's ten best category A races and further amendments to the format were made in later years. Since the 1986 season, an English Fell Running Championships series has also taken place, based on results in various races of different lengths over the year.

Race times vary from a few minutes to a few hours. The longest common fell running challenges tend to be rounds to be completed within 24 hours, such as the Bob Graham Round[5] which was first completed in 1932. Some of the mountain marathons call for pairs of runners to carry equipment and food for camping overnight.

In addition to the Guides Races, popular events in the Lake District include Fairfield Horseshoe, Skiddaw, Kentmere Horseshoe and Wansfell and, further south, the Three Peaks race in North Yorkshire which ascends the fells of Pen-y-ghent, Whernside and Ingleborough on a course of over 23 miles, starting and finishing in Horton-in-Ribblesdale.

Joss Naylor, a sheep farmer from Wasdale Head is generally regarded as the 'father' of modern fell running. His speciality was long distance challenges like the Bob Graham Round which he extended to the highest number of peaks he could cover within 24 hours, setting records in the 1970s, when he was in his thirties, which culminated in his traverse of 72 peaks involving a distance of over 100 miles (160 km) and 37,000 feet (11,000 m) of ascent in 23 hours 20 minutes. Chris Brasher, the Olympic Gold medallist, journalist, broadcaster and founder of the London Marathon regarded Naylor as 'The Greatest of Them All'.

Naylor's 'heir apparent' was Billy Bland from Borrowdale who, along with his brothers and wider family[5A], also specialised in long distance challenges. Bland set a record of 13 hours 53 minutes for the standard peaks of the Bob Graham Round in 1982, which stood for 32 years. His life story, 'All Or Nothing at All: The Life of Billy Bland', by Steve Chilton, was published in 2020.

JOSS NAYLOR IN ACTION IN HIS HEYDAY (Photographer unknown)

Dave Cannon of Kendal, Jeff Norman from Leigh in Lancashire, and Kenny Stuart of Threlkeld were prolific fell running champions and course record holders who, later in their careers, became marathon runners of the highest international class. Cannon, who was Fell Runner of the Year in 1972, and won the annual Ben Nevis race five times in the 1970s, finished first equal in the Paris marathon in 1981 and had a best time of 2 hours 11 minutes and 21 seconds.

Stuart, who began his fell running career on the professional circuit, was a multiple champion in the early 1980s and set records in several classic fell races including Skiddaw, Ben Nevis and Snowdon. He recorded a time of 2:11:36 in the Houston Marathon in 1989, in finishing in second place. Stuart's intense, almost legendary, rivalry with John Wild from South Derbyshire, who was a leading track and field and cross country international before taking up fell running, is recounted in Steve Chilton's book, *'Running Hard: the story of a rivalry'*, published in 2017. Norman, who won the Three Peaks six times in the 1970s, competed for Britain in the marathon at the Montreal Olympic Games in 1976.

The successes of these runners belied the notion that fell running was somehow an easy, specialist option which was inferior to international track, road or cross country distance running.

With the advent of mass participation in running, many more events have cropped up in the Lakes and trail running has become especially popular in recent years, coinciding with the increased participation of runners of all standards, in a similar way to road races such as 5k parkruns, 10ks and half marathons. Trail running generally takes place on well-defined paths or tracks which are relatively easy to follow, precluding the need for map reading, and do not involve the significant amounts of ascent that are required in fell running, or indeed the need to reach summits.

These relatively new events are generally for individuals, rather than for club teams, and have become very commercial through promoters such as Lakeland Trails, which organises trail races throughout the region, with the entrance fees including for incentives such as event T shirts, bottles of water and chocolate snacks for every competitor at the end of the race.

On typical summer weekends, many events including fell races, trail races and road races are held in the Lake District. However, despite the popularity of these challenges, it is not particularly common to see athletes out on the fells on a training run. There are still many more walkers.

[3]This time was equalled in 1983 by John Wild.

[4]The Ascent Categories consist of:

Category A
- Should average not less than 50 metres climb per kilometre.
- Should not have more than 20% of the race distance on road.
- Should be at least 1.5 kilometres in length.

Category B
- Should average not less than 25 metres climb per kilometre.
- Should not have more than 30% of the race distance on road.

Category C
- Should average not less than 20 metres climb per kilometre.
- Should not have more than 40% of the race distance on road.
- Should contain some genuine fell terrain.

There are other, separate categories based on distance, orienteering-style challenges and multi-day events.

[5] The **Bob Graham Round** is named after Bob Graham (1889–1966), a Keswick guest-house owner who, in June 1932, traversed 42 specific fells within a 24-hour period. The Round was first repeated, in a faster time, in 1960 by Alan Heaton. The current record time by a male is 12hr 52m set in 2018 by the Catalan runner, Kilian Jornet. The women's record is 15hr 24m, set by Jasmin Paris from Derbyshire, in 2016.

[5A] Pete Bland was another well known member of the Bland dynasty, and winner of the fell race at Ambleside Sports in 1968. However, he was best known as the owner of 'Pete Bland Sports', based in Kendal, and his red retail van was a regular attendee at fell races throughout the north of England. Pete was revered as a tireless organiser and official in local and national fell running circles for over forty years. He died aged 79 of coronavirus in November 2020.

GENERAL ADVICE

TRAINING TECHNIQUES

The degree of training you are aiming for will vary hugely from runner to runner, jogger to jogger depending on the level of competitiveness you want to achieve either in terms of your own performances, or against other athletes.

At one end of the scale will be the 100 miles a week athlete, perhaps striving to be competitive at the national level, and at the other you may not want to be competitive at all, merely be interested in running or jogging for the sheer enjoyment of the activity itself. This book is mainly concerned with the less serious runners who want to challenge themselves but have no ambitions (at least, not in the first instance) beyond that. Some readers may find that they are natural athletes and may decide to train and compete at a higher level as they get fitter.

For the competitors you need to decide what target you want to achieve in the short, medium and longer terms. Should you run every day, perhaps even twice a day, or do you need to take days off in between to make sure you are properly rested, whether mentally or physically, between runs?

If you haven't run seriously before you will need to make sure you are free of any underlying problems and a health check and advice from a doctor may be prudent, particularly if you have had health issues in the past. It's important to recognise your own degree of fitness at the beginning, start modestly and work up to a realistic level of training for the performance level which suits you best.

Training options include longer 'steady' runs, interval running, fartlek and hill repetitions and a mixture of all of these can be built into a serious (or perhaps not so serious) training programme.

Steady Runs: Steady runs are continuous runs over longer distances at more or less the same speed, which build aerobic capacity.

Interval Running: Interval running is primarily of anaerobic benefit. A typical session might involve running at speed for 400 metres, resting or jogging in between for two minutes, and then repeating the exercise, say, eight times.

In my experience it is not advisable to push yourself to complete exhaustion when interval training. Always finish a session feeling that you have something in reserve. This is of psychological benefit, builds confidence, and avoids a feeling of dread when the next session comes around.

Interval running can be a very quick way of gaining fitness, but it needs to be supplemented with alternate days of steady, aerobic running in order for your fitness level to be sustainable.

Fartlek: This is a Swedish term meaning 'speed play' which originated in the late 1930s in Sweden. The world records for several distances from 1,500 metres to 5,000 metres, set during World War II by Gunder Hägg, Arne Andersson and others, were largely attributed to fartlek training. It involves continuous runs with periods of speed work over distances varying, say, between 100 metres and 1,000 metres, alternating with jogging, ideally over shorter distances, in between, and can be performed on any kind of terrain.

Fartlek has the advantage of developing both aerobic and anaerobic fitness levels at the same time, and it avoids the repetitiveness of interval running which can lead to mental staleness, especially if it is carried out on a running track.

In any event, running through the countryside will often be broken up into sections of varying length as matter of course, due to the diverse terrain.

Hill Repetitions: This is basically 'fartlek on an incline', with uphill runs (of, say, between 100 metres and 300 metres, depending on the severity of the incline) at effort with a jog downhill and back to the start in between, repeated like an interval session.

If you are restricted to using the same incline for each of your uphill strides, the downhill jog can be executed with more effort than normal in order to reduce the time, in lieu of the distance, between. Through experience you will be able to work out what level of effort suits you best.

Here are some examples of a balanced training programme. These have been related to base levels of performance on the road as it is not possible to compare off-road courses, particularly over fell or trails. In order to achieve the target times, a build-up period of approximately 8 weeks should be allowed for:

Age Range:	16-19
Existing Experience:	None
Initial Target time for 5k road run:	20 minutes

Sunday –	8k steady trail run
Monday –	5k fartlek on grass/trail consisting of a warm-up of approximately 800m metres, 6 strides of between 300 metres and 600 metres with a jog of two thirds of each distance between, and a warm down jog of 800 metres.
Tuesday –	Rest
Wednesday –	Hill repetitions consisting of 800 metres warm up jog; 8 x 200 metres uphill strides, with jog downhill to the start in between; 800 metres warm down jog
Thursday –	5k easy trail run
Friday –	Rest
Saturday –	Race or the equivalent of a 5k steady road run in 22 minutes

Age Range:	20-24
Existing Experience:	None
Initial Target time for 5k road run:	25 minutes

Sunday –	8k steady trail run
Monday –	Rest
Tuesday –	5k fartlek on grass/trail consisting of a warmup jog of 500 metres, 8 strides of approximately 300 metres with a slow 200 metres between each, and a warm down jog of 500 metres
Wednesday –	Rest
Thursday –	5k easy trail run
Friday –	Rest
Saturday –	Race or the equivalent of a 5k steady road run in 27 minutes

Age Range:	40-44
Existing Experience:	Regular fun runner, non-competitive
Initial Target time for 5k road run:	25 minutes

Sunday –	10k steady trail run/jog
Monday –	Rest
Tuesday –	Warm up jog of 1k; 6 x 300 metres interval strides on grass with 200 metres jog between; warm down jog of 500 metres.
Wednesday –	Rest
Thursday –	easy road run
Friday –	Rest
Saturday –	Race or 5k hard, steady trail run

Age Range:	50-54
Existing Experience:	Long term competitor
Initial Target time for 5k road run:	20 minutes

Sunday –	12k steady trail run
Monday –	Warm up jog of 1k; 6 x 300 metres interval strides on grass with 200 metres jog between; warm down jog of 500 metres.
Tuesday –	Rest
Wednesday –	5k fartlek on grass consisting of a warmup jog of 500 metres, 8 strides of approximately 300 metres with a slow 200 metres between each, and a warm down jog of 500 metres
Thursday –	5k steady road run
Friday –	Rest
Saturday –	Race or 8k steady trail run

COMPETITION

When it comes to competition, the general principle is to continue training hard in the first half of a race week and to taper off in the last two days before the event. Don't be too concerned if you can't seem to achieve your targets in training as the 'adrenaline rush' of an event will normally boost your competitive performances as a matter of course.

A hard 5k training run on the road will convert into a performance approximately one minute faster in a race. By maintaining and increasing your fitness level, running at a good pace will become easier the longer you have been doing it and, through time, once-difficult runs will become relaxing and much more enjoyable.

It's important, too, to warm up before a run, with a slow jog of at least five minutes and, in a competitive situation, with several fast strides of, say, 50 metres, in order to elevate your heart rate and gear up your muscles before the race starts. A proper warm-up also allows you to prepare yourself mentally for the effort ahead and a slow jog and some stretching afterwards will help you to avoid injuries and keep you in shape for the next time.

With regard to running technique, do not become too hidebound about the way you run, just carry on with what is natural to yourself. Technique obviously becomes very important in distinguishing between sprinting, middle distance running and marathons on the road, especially at the elite level, but that is not the concern of this book.

A shorter stride length reduces impact on each stride but obviously increases the number of strides you take. Downhill running does demand a certain technique but is more often than not down to whoever is prepared to take the greatest risk of ankle injuries and falls.

And remember, Emil Zatopek, arguably the greatest distance runner of the twentieth century, was not exactly the prettiest athlete on two legs. "I shall learn to have a better style," he said, "once they start judging races according to their beauty."

CLOTHING AND FOOTWEAR

There is a huge amount of choice nowadays and specialist running outlets, albeit with commercial interests, will advise you on the best options for different scenarios without you having to spend huge amounts of money.

In summer, shorts and T shirts are adequate and don't require much advice. However, winter training, especially on open country does require some deliberation. Full tracksuits are essential, with at least one layer underneath. The layers create gaps between which increase the insulation level, in the same way as cavity wall construction in buildings. Cotton is a good insulant but it absorbs more sweat which becomes very cold if you have to stop. In these instances, a base layer of man-made fibre is a better option as it draws sweat away from the body and allows the moisture to evaporate.

Hats, gloves and neck tubes also help to maintain body temperature in winter. And don't be put off by a cold, wet and dark winter night. With the right clothing you should feel as warm as toast within ten minutes of starting a run, with any lethargy well and truly dispelled. You will feel wonderful afterwards, providing you don't hang around in the cold after finishing your run, and it can be surprising how rarely you get soaked through.

Your choice of shoes should match the terrain you are running on, whether over trails, fell or roads. Again, there is endless choice in the running outlets, with staff who are trained to advise you on shoes which suit your running style and the types of runs you have in mind. However, you may find that it is difficult to discover runs over country that don't involve differing surfaces and good judgement is required on what shoes are best in the circumstances. While this is of little consequence on training runs it's important to have a reasonable idea of the terrain in a trail or fell race. I once wore studded shoes in a cross-country race which gave me an advantage over the country but were a disaster on the section of wet road at the end which the organisers hadn't told us about!

SUSTENANCE

Carrying water is not necessary on most of the runs outlined here, or in shorter races of under 30 minutes, and can be an unnecessary hindrance, restricting movement and compromising balance. However, you should follow the dictum that you should drink water if you feel thirsty. Make sure you are well (but not over) hydrated before racing but avoid drinking anything other than water too close to a race as it may cause stomach pains or a stitch.

It's important to recognise the difference between a race and a training run when deciding when to eat. A stitch or a bloated feeling on a training run can be managed easily by slowing down or stopping and massaging, or just putting up with it. But you should to try to avoid stitches altogether in a serious race where all your concentration needs to be focused on the maximum physical effort in the circumstances.

Don't eat too close to a training or fun run. A small snack at least one hour beforehand should be fine but if you are planning a large meal during the day, or in the evening, get your run in first.

On a race day, snack only beforehand. If the race is in the morning, get up early and have a light breakfast at least two hours before the event. If it is later in the day avoid overeating, sticking to small snacks not less than two hours before the race. Again, through time, as you gain experience, you will be able to work out what suits you as an individual best.

MANAGING INJURIES

From time to time you will experience injuries particularly, but not exclusively, to your legs, feet, groin or hip. If an injury is caused by a fall or an accident during your normal daily regime you can be pretty sure, subject to the severity of the injury, that it will clear up in time and you will be able to get back to running. Even a broken leg heals. However, injuries to muscles and tendons caused by running itself are sometimes more exasperating to manage, and can be difficult to cope with mentally as you have no idea how long they might persist for.

As a young athlete I experienced shin soreness (technically, 'medial tibial stress syndrome'), which appeared to be caused by covering high mileages, mostly on roads, wearing inadequate footwear. Through experience I worked out that ten days of complete rest were necessary (a week was not enough, resulting in me 'going back to square one'), and the recovery period involved running only on grass, which became my optimum training surface, with heel cushioning inserted in my shoes.

The first rule to apply when an injury comes on is to be cautious and stop running if necessary. Sometimes a minor niggle on a training run can become a long-term injury if you try to continue. In the first instance, the current advice is to apply the rules of **RICE**, namely:

Rest the injured part as much as possible to allow healing of damaged tissues.

Apply **Ice** wrapped in a damp towel for 10 minutes every 2 hours.

Apply a **Compression** bandage to help minimise the swelling of the tissues.

Elevate your leg to help limit blood flow to, and prevent the use of, the affected muscles.

It is important that the RICE regime is followed for at least the first 48 to 72 hours after injury.

If the injury persists you should seek advice from an appropriate professional such as a physiotherapist. They will be able to diagnose the injury, provide you with details of daily exercises to speed your recovery, and advise you, and hopefully encourage you, on your prognosis.

Be sensible about how long to stay off training once injured. The length of time you take to return to your original level of fitness will vary from individual to individual but if you are generally fit anyway this should involve less than 50% of the time out injured. Other non-impact exercise such as swimming or cycling, including stationary cycling, will help to maintain fitness.

When you feel ready, start very slowly, increasing your effort day by day if the injury problem seems to have been resolved. Massage to the injured area using embrocation before running and the application of ice afterwards will also provide physical support and inspire confidence in your recovery process. Older runners with experience are more likely to know how to avoid injury but may take longer to recover once they are injured. They also tend to have poorer circulation and therefore will get slight muscular niggles which get worse if they continue to run, and can only be resolved by rest and stretching exercises.

The advantage of trail running is that there is less impact on the softer surfaces. Heel cushioning will also help to reduce impact. The drawback is that uneven ground, or slippy surfaces, may result in twisted ankles or muscle strains. It is therefore important to concentrate and stay alert to where you are putting your feet in certain circumstances, for example when running over tree roots or across stony ground.

Slow jog warm-ups and warm-downs, and stretching exercises after runs, will help to ensure that you avoid similar injuries in the future.

SAFETY

Don't assume that, just because the runs illustrated here are short and over relatively accessible terrain, you don't need to say where you're going before you leave (for example, by posting a note on your car), and you should wear the right clothes for the time of year. It may be advisable, too, to take a mobile phone with you, allowing you to make contact with people if you run into difficulty.

Unlike track or road running, variations in weather conditions can significantly alter the time taken, even on standard routes. You may carry your phone in any case to record and monitor your runs, but don't allow statistics to overrule the sheer pleasure of running in open country free of pressure, with great views, over varied and interesting terrain.

Unless you feel particularly confident, stick to your planned trail and bear in mind that trail running is mostly on uneven ground, carrying the possibility of the trips, falls and twisted ankles which can affect everyone regardless of their fitness level. You should also avoid starting a run too late in the day over unlit territory but, if you do, take a headlamp with you, and be prepared to slow down to walking pace if circumstances demand. Wear a 'hi vis' or equivalent top (a white T shirt will suffice), especially in winter or if you are running on vehicular roads.

Extra clothing may have to be carried on longer runs in the winter, in case you have to abandon the run due to injury or a fall, since your body temperature will drop quickly once you stop running resulting, in extreme cases, in hypothermia. In these situations try to keep walking if you can't run. But, rather than becoming too alarmed about this possibility, bear in mind that this is very unlikely to happen on the types of runs illustrated in this book, which will rarely extend beyond one hour.

HEALTH AND WELL-BEING

Running has always been considered a competitive pursuit. From early days at school, children have competed at runs round the playground or the local park as they strive for the kudos of being the fastest runner in the class. Competitive track and field athletics became fully formalised in Victorian times with the setting up, in Britain, of the Amateur Athletics Association in 1880, as the first national body for the sport, and with the advent of the first modern Olympic Games in Athens in 1896.

However, it has always been taken for granted that there is much more to running than the purely competitive element, although not necessarily in an evidence-based way. It is now recognised that running, in particular, engages most parts of the human body in high-impact movements and that exercise increases your heart rate, burns calories, and strengthens legs and core and, to a lesser extent, arm muscles, and will help to stabilise ankles.

Each person will have their own take on what distances they can cover and what pace they can achieve while running. However, regardless of natural ability, the more you run, the greater capacity your lungs will have, resulting in greater stamina and the ability to recover more quickly after exercise. Moreover, running on a regular basis can prevent certain diseases such as stroke, diabetes and heart disease and it burns a lot of calories, which can contribute to weight loss and, through time, to a consistent, healthy, weight level, helping to lower blood pressure, and blood sugar and blood cholesterol levels.

If you can run free of discomfort it can give you the reassurance that there's not much wrong with your health and can be a good early warning system if you are unfortunate enough to experience heart and lung problems. However, if you are not a regular runner, or indeed have never run since your schooldays, you should seek medical advice before taking it up, especially if you have a history of health concerns[6].

In more recent years, the psychological benefits of running to mental health and well-being have also become acknowledged and have almost become a significant justification for taking up running in the first place, or for continuing to run after a competitive career in sport. It can even provide, in many cases, a wholesome and easily accessible alternative to medication.

These benefits include increased mental clarity, a boost in energy, and improved sleep. Running stimulates the brain chemicals serotonin, dopamine and endorphins which make you feel relaxed and happy, improving self-esteem and engendering confidence through feeling fit. These chemical releases also contribute to an increase in your energy levels, with more oxygen being delivered to your tissues, improving sustainability.

There is no doubt that running can address the need to unwind from the stress-inducing pressures of modern living. In particular, running at a pace which still allows you to talk while running, and maintain a conversation in the company of others, means you are not over stressing on your run and are at the same time benefitting from social interaction. By no means need it become a competitive activity. However, running on your own, at your own preferred pace, can also be a good way to clear your head and perhaps help to resolve problems which are causing stress.

The environment in which you run can be important too, with the park or the countryside, and indeed trails and fells, potentially better options than urban surroundings. Running helps you to cover more ground and to observe a greater area of countryside and wildlife. For competitive athletes, running can also provide long term benefits to your ability to cope with pressure in other situations in your life.

---

[6] There have more recently been some concerns about the correlation between extreme exercise and illnesses such as stroke, atrial fibrillation and heart disease. Martin Duff, a long-term contributor to Athletics Weekly and a former World Veterans Marathon Champion, has recently conducted research into the potential for heart disease in later life arising from high intensity training in younger days.

The one clear piece of advice on health for serious competitive athletes is to avoid training through colds, flu, viruses or other temporary illnesses which can cause excessive strain on the heart. However, it is not fully known what the recommended limits of extreme exercise should be and you should bear in mind that questions about health arising from training to excess are far removed from regular, easy jogging or running 'within yourself', where quite the opposite effects are cited.

A COMPETITOR ON RESTON SCAR IN THE LAKELAND TRAILS EVENT 2018
(© Jumpy James)
www.jumpyjames.co.uk

THE TRAILS

All the trails described involve loops which take you back to the start of your run, thus eliminating the need for complicated manoeuvres with regard to transport. South Lakes is also well served by buses and the Lakes Line train service between Oxenholme and Windermere, and the availability, where feasible, of public transport is mentioned under each of the descriptions.

The trails are divided into areas within South Lakeland – North, West, Central, East and South - and are arranged in order of severity, from relatively mild to relatively arduous, within each area. The areas are designated according to the Ordnance Survey map co-ordinates for the starting points for each run, rather than local names, which are instead used in the descriptions of the trails themselves,

Instructions for locating the starting points are used as a guide only, and assume that you are based in the South Lakes area at the time. However, most people will use a map or satellite navigation for this purpose.

Although references to distance, time and ascent for each trail have been included the emphasis here is on the sense of freedom, the scenery and the enjoyment of the activity for its own sake. Besides, most runners and joggers will introduce a competitive element for themselves if that is how they are so-minded, and many will use Apps, such as MapMyRun and Strava, as a matter of course. It should be noted, however, that the times indicated under each trail are a general guide only and assume a good level of fitness across the age groups.

Another obvious but nevertheless important point to bear in mind is that, unlike road running, the conditions on these trails will vary greatly depending on the seasons. A pleasant run on a grassy path in summer may become slippy, muddy and often unforgiving in the winter.

LOCATION OF TRAILS

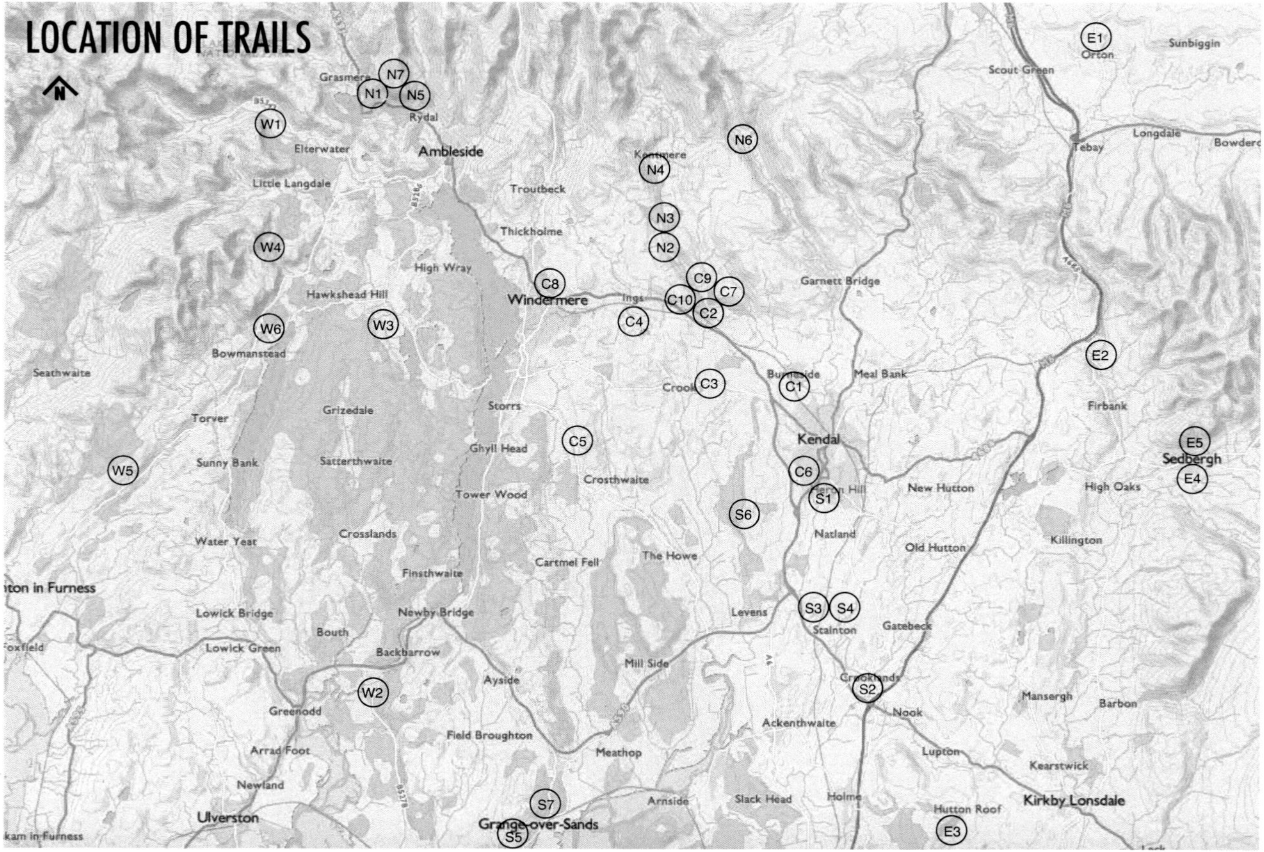

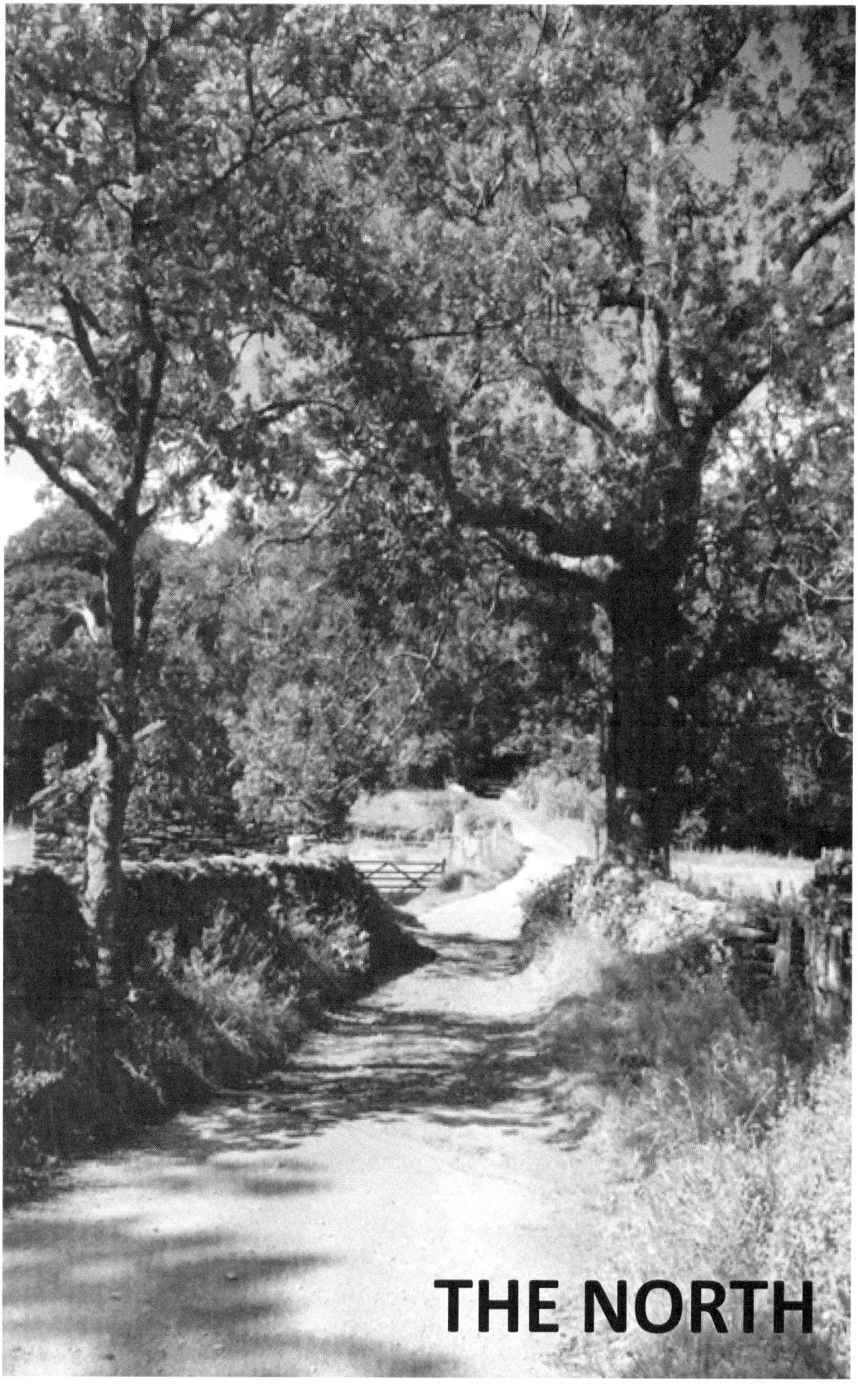
THE NORTH

Trail N1: The Grasmere Lake Round

Grasmere Lake is very popular with casual walkers who enjoy the shoreline with its dramatic views of the surrounding fells. William Wordsworth lived at Dove Cottage in Grasmere from 1799 until he moved to Rydal Mount in 1813. He is buried in the cemetery at St Oswald's Church in the village.

The trail can be combined with Trail N5 to provide an overall distance of 12.5km/8.0 miles. There are several options for parking throughout the run which are useful for varying your starting point on future occasions.

The start of this trail is accessible by the 555 Stagecoach bus which travels between Kendal and Keswick.

Approximate Distance:	8.0 km/5.0 miles
Terrain:	Road surfaces and constructed paths, with a short section over meadow.
Severity:	Several inclines on the sections of paved country lane, interspersed with easy running on level paths.
Approximate Time:	35-50 minutes
Total Ascent:	172m.
Start of the Trail:	From Ambleside, drive north on the A591 passing Rydal Water until you see White Moss car park on the left. Carry on for a short distance and turn right into the pay car park on the other side of the road.
Map Reference:	NY 348 066 (OS Explorer Map OL7: South-Eastern Lakes – North Sheet)

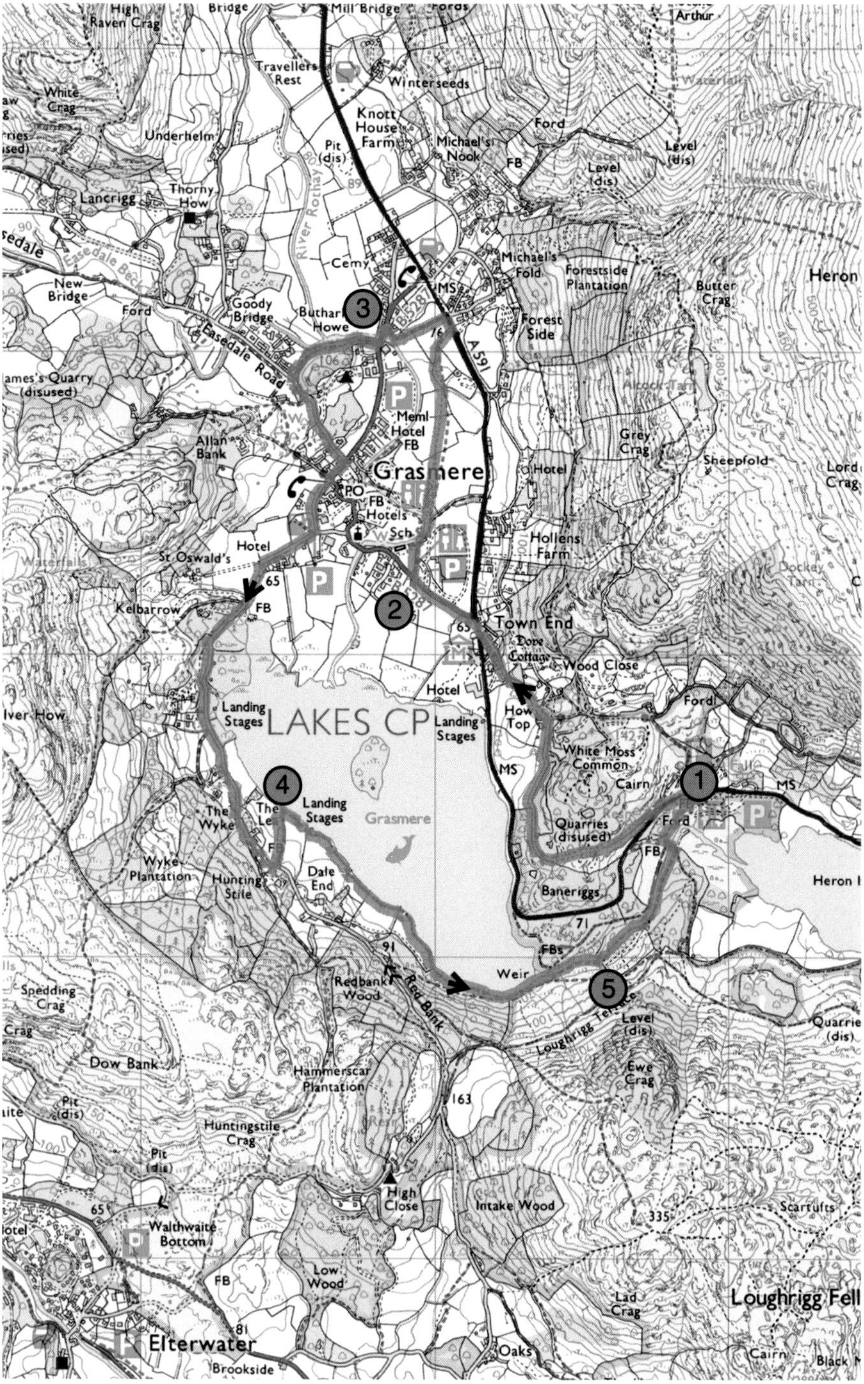
Grasmere
LAKES CP
Town End
Dove Cottage
White Moss Common
Loughrigg Terrace
Loughrigg Fell
Elterwater
Redbank Wood
Hammerscar Plantation
Intake Wood
High Close
1
2
3
4
5

1 Set out from the car park in the direction of Grasmere, passing the pay meter to reach a narrow paved lane. Carry on along the undulating lane for approximately 1500 metres. There is very little vehicular traffic here and there is no need to be too cautious. The lane sweeps left, then right, skirting the quarries below White Moss Common, and you will soon reach a downhill section to Town End and the new slate building next to the Wordsworth Centre. Use the crossing over the main A591 to reach Stock Lane (B5287), heading into Grasmere from the south. Run on the right-hand side of the road for 250 metres until you see the footpath sign immediately beyond the public car park on the right.

2 Follow the clear path as it merges with the River Rothay, until you reach the footbridge on the left. Do not cross the bridge but instead carry straight on, passing through a gate with a signpost for the A591 (700 yards). Cross the meadow, passing through gates on the way and curving to the right at the end as you head up to the main road. Turn left after negotiating the gate and left again after a few metres, following the signage at a narrow, enclosed path which bends to the right at the end to reach the B5287 into Grasmere from the north.

3 Turn left onto the road, cross the road bridge over the Rothay and look for the footpath on the right-hand side which directs you into the wooded area of Butharlyp Howe. Run up the steep path and round the hill to join the Easdale Road, and follow this to the left to reach Broadgate in the centre of the village, just beyond the Heaton Cooper Gallery.

Turn right onto Broadgate, heading away from the centre, and continue on for a short distance until you reach the junction with Red Bank Road. Turn right again and follow this road as it departs the village and climbs towards Elterwater and Loughrigg. Look for a bend left and then right after about 1500 metres and you will see signage taking you off road on the left to follow a reconstructed path which heads downhill to the lake.

4 Follow the path along the lakeside enjoying the scenery and the magnificent trees. As the wooded area ends, pass through a gate and head along the shoreline to the footbridge over the River Rothay. Do not cross the bridge but continue on the right-hand side of the river, taking care to protect your ankles as you run along a reconstructed path of river stones. (Alternatively, you can cross the footbridge, turning right to follow the path downhill on the other side of the Rothay.)

5 The path shortly reaches a gate into White Moss woodland and continues down along the side of the Rothay until you reach a modern footbridge. Cross the bridge and continue on the other side of the river, looking for a path off to the left which will take you up some roughly constructed stone steps to reach the busy A591. Be extremely careful crossing here as the sight lines are limited and the road has double white lines. However, there is no urgency as your run is effectively over with the car park immediately across the road.

THE FOOTBRIDGE OVER THE RIVER ROTHAY AT THE SOUTHERN END OF GRASMERE LAKE
(The Author)

Trail N2: Kentmere and the Daffodil Moor

This trail replicates much of the terrain you may experience in a short fell race. From Ulthwaite Bridge over the River Kent, it climbs onto the moorland below Sour Howes and Sallows, returning by farm tracks and a paved country lane.

Approximate Distance:	6.75 km/4.25 miles.
Terrain:	Mostly paths and tracks, with a mixture of rocky and grassy sections, and a long descent on the paved country lane at the end of the run.
Severity:	Steady climb for the first two kilometres, and level running through open fields and along farm tracks, ending with the steep downhill on the road.
Approximate Time:	35-50 minutes.
Total Ascent:	184m.
Start of the Trail:	Drive north from Staveley on the Kentmere Road, crossing Scroggs Bridge over the River Kent, about half a mile from the outskirts of the village. Continue for another mile and a half or so until you see Ulthwaite Bridge on the left. Park on the area of ground just beyond the junction with the farm track which passes across the bridge.
Map Reference:	NY 456 012 (OS Explorer Map OL7: South-Eastern Lakes – North Sheet)

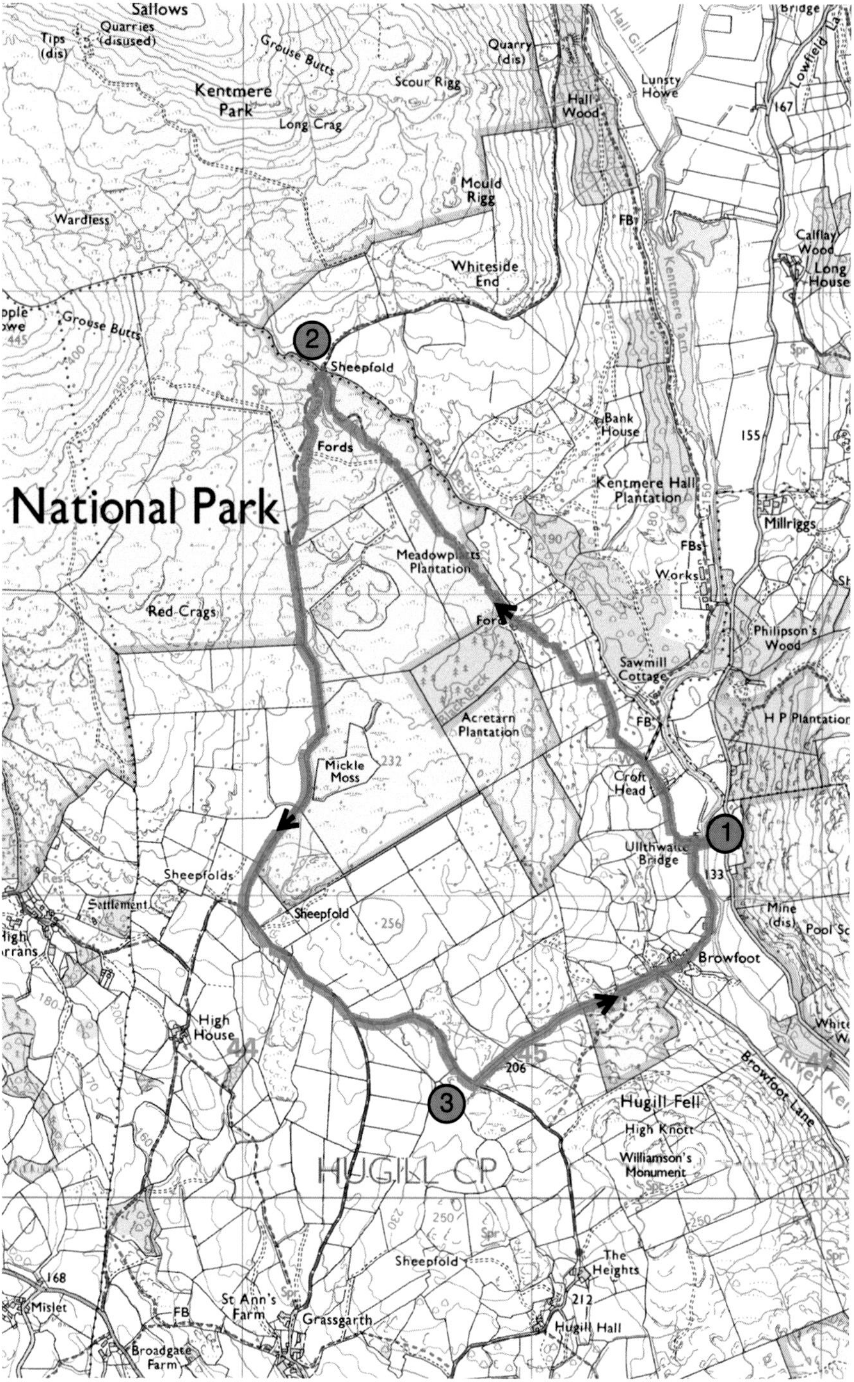
Sallows
Tips (dis)
Quarries (disused)
Grouse Butts
Quarry (dis)
Hall Gill
Scour Rigg
Kentmere Park
Long Crag
Hall Wood
Lunsty Howe
Lowfield La
167
Mould Rigg
Wardless
FB
Calflay Wood
Long House
Whiteside End
Kentmere Tarn
Grouse Butts
445
2
Sheepfold
Spr
Fords
Bank House
155
Kentmere Hall Plantation
National Park
Meadowplatts Plantation
190
Millriggs
FBs
Works
Red Crags
Ford
Philipson's Wood
Sawmill Cottage
Black Beck
Acretarn Plantation
FB
H P Plantation
Mickle Moss
232
Croft Head
1
Ullthwaite Bridge
133
Sheepfolds
Settlement
Sheepfold
256
Mine (dis)
Pool Sc
Browfoot
High House
206
Browfoot Lane
River Kent
3
Hugill Fell
High Knott
Williamson's Monument
HUGILL CP
250
Sheepfold
The Heights
168
Mislet
FB
St Ann's Farm
Grassgarth
212
Hugill Hall
Broadgate Farm

1 Set out from the car park, passing over Ulthwaite Bridge, and follow the enclosed farm track which takes a sharp right after about a hundred metres. Continue on this path through the gate between the houses at Croft Head. Continue on the main path which becomes more of a well-worn single track passing through several farm gates. The track soon becomes rock-strewn as it climbs steeply towards Kentmere Park and Sallows.

After about one kilometre you will pass a derelict shepherd's cottage on the left and shortly afterwards a ford over Black Beck. Pace yourself on this section and carry on through two further gates up the steep, grassy and undulating ascent to the plateau of the daffodil moor where you will eventually reach another ford over Park Beck.

2 Turn left at this point, crossing the ford, and follow the mountain biking trail heading southwards over the daffodil moor to the gate in the far-right corner. Go through the gate, keeping to the path with a wall on your left. Continue on this muddy section through two further gates bounding an enclosure.

After negotiating the second of these gates, continue on the same path, with the wall now on the right, and follow the winding track for approximately one kilometre, through further gates until you reach a signposted junction of farm tracks. Go left at this point onto the enclosed track and at the next junction take the left-hand fork and continue on for a short distance to reach the top of the small country lane up from Browfoot Farm.

3 Run down the steep incline on the lane until you reach the signposted path to Browfoot, ignoring the alternative route just before this junction. Follow the path through Browfoot as it swings left at the River Kent and takes you back on a rocky path to Ulthwaite Bridge and the start of the run.

SETTING OUT ACROSS ULTHWAITE BRIDGE
(The Author)

Trail N3: The Kentmere Hall Loop

The first part of this trail follows the same route as Trail N2, climbing onto the moorland below Sallows before descending to Kentmere Hall, a 14th century tunnel-vaulted pele tower. Of the original tower, only the turrets, one of the original windows, and the spiral staircase remain. The tower was extended in the 15th and 16th centuries into a residence and is now a farmhouse.

Kentmere Hall's claim to fame is that Bernard Gilpin was born there in 1517. Gilpin was a famous preacher in Henry VIII's time and a leading churchman during the reign of Mary Tudor. He became a Fellow at Queen's College, Oxford, Rector of Thornton-le-Moors, Vicar of Norton, Rector of Houghton-le-Spring and Archdeacon of Durham. He was known as the "Apostle of the North". There are several local references to his family name, including Gilpin Farm and Gilpin Hotel near Crook.

The path back to the start of this trail passes through a factory which is currently a heating, ventilating and air conditioning business. It was originally the home of Kentmere Limited which produced photographic paper and is now a packaging company based in Staveley.

Approximate Distance:	8.0 km/5.0 miles
Terrain:	Paths almost throughout, with a mixture of rocky and grassy sections.
Severity:	Steady climb for the first two kilometres, followed by an undulating farm track and a steep downhill towards Kentmere Hall, and relatively easy thereafter.
Approximate Time:	40-60 minutes.
Total Ascent:	236m.
Start of the Trail:	Drive north from Staveley on the Kentmere Road, crossing Scroggs Bridge over the River Kent, about half a mile from the outskirts of the village. Continue for another mile and a half or so until you see Ulthwaite Bridge on the left. Park on the area of ground just beyond the junction with the farm track which passes over the bridge.
Map Reference:	NY 456 012 (OS Explorer Map OL7: South-Eastern Lakes – North Sheet)

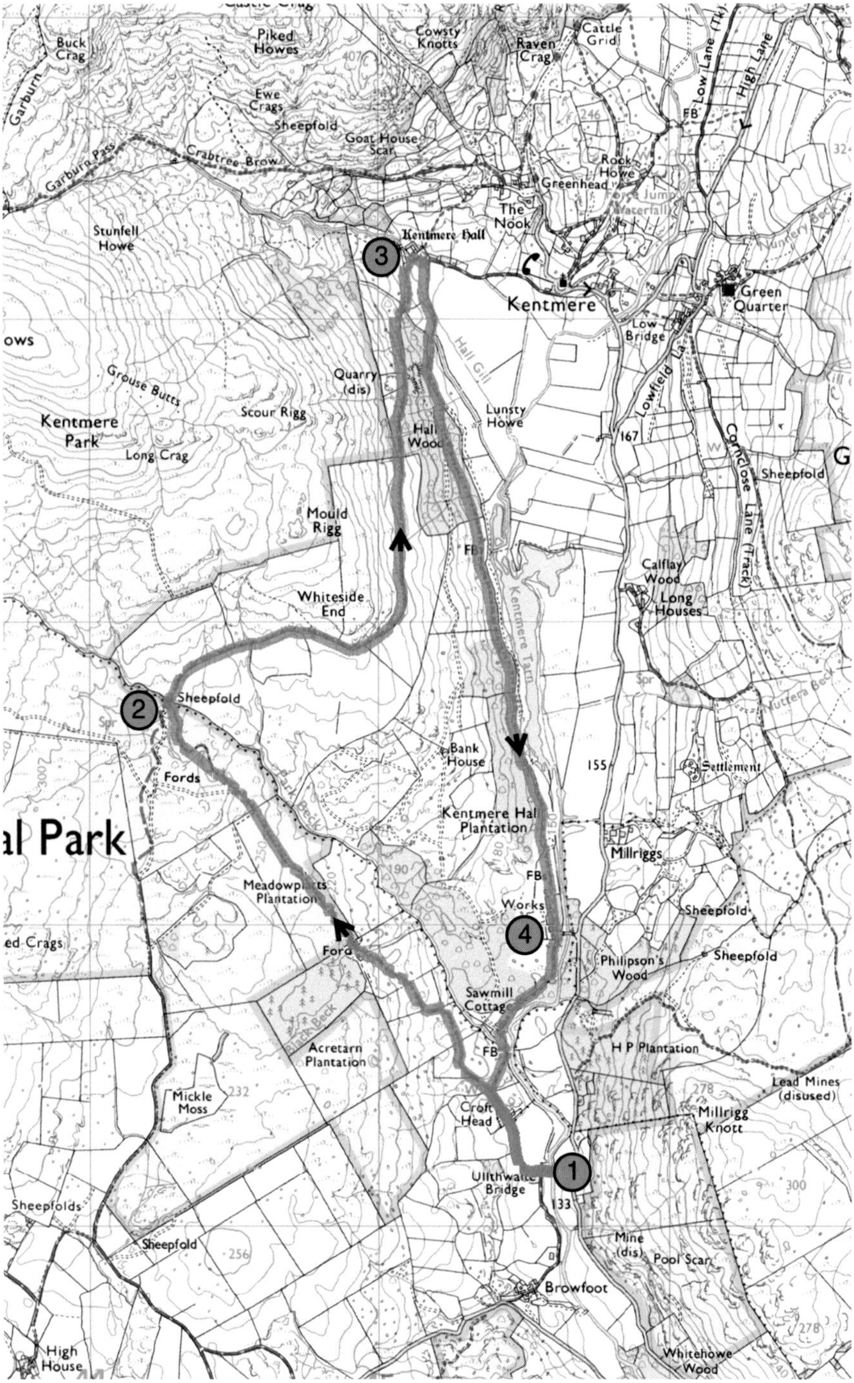
Buck Crag
Piked Howes
Cowsty Knotts
Raven Crag
Cattle Grid
Ewe Crags
Sheepfold
Goat House Scar
Crabtree Brow
Garburn Pass
Rook Howe
Greenhead
Stunfell Howe
The Nook
Kentmere Hall
Kentmere
Green Quarter
Low Bridge
Grouse Butts
Quarry (dis)
Hall Gill
Kentmere Park
Scour Rigg
Long Crag
Lunsty Howe
Hall Wood
Lowfield La
Corn Close Lane (Track)
Sheepfold
Mould Rigg
FB
Calflay Wood
Long Houses
Whiteside End
Kentmere Tarn
Sheepfold
Bank House
Settlement
Fords
Kentmere Hall Plantation
Millriggs
al Park
Meadowplatts Plantation
FB
Works
Sheepfold
Philipson's Wood
Sheepfold
Ford
Sawmill Cottage
Acretarn Plantation
FB
H P Plantation
Lead Mines (disused)
Mickle Moss
Croft Head
Millrigg Knott
Ulthwaite Bridge
Sheepfolds
Sheepfold
Mine (dis)
Pool Scar
Browfoot
High House
Whitehowe Wood
1
2
3
4

1 Set out from the car park over the bridge and follow the enclosed farm track which takes a sharp right after about a hundred metres. Continue on this path through the gate between the houses at Croft Head. You will pass the path on the right which brings you back to the start of the run but continue ahead on the main path which becomes more of a well-worn single track passing through several farm gates. The track soon becomes rock-strewn as it climbs steeply towards Kentmere Park and Sallows.

After about one kilometre you will pass a shepherd's cottage on the left and, shortly afterwards, a ford over Black Beck. Pace yourself on this section and carry on through two further gates up the steep, grassy and undulating ascent to the plateau of the daffodil moor where you will eventually reach another ford over Park Beck.

2 Do not cross the ford but instead go through the field gate to the right and, after passing a sheep fold, take another gate to the right which leads you onto a farm track. The track passes through several gates, eventually sweeping left down the steep hill to Kentmere Hall. The descent offers a panoramic view of the village of Kentmere, with its prominent St Cuthbert's Church, and the pretty hamlet of Green Quarter beyond to the east.

3 Turn right onto the farm access road at the bottom of the hill, next to Kentmere Hall, and, following the sign, take another right after a hundred metres through a field gate and onto the path which leads you back to the start of the run. Take the right-hand path where it forks and continue up and over the short incline through Hall Wood.

Although there are some stiles and gates to negotiate this path is undulating, occasionally grassy and generally downhill, allowing you to stretch your legs following the exertions of the steep climb to the daffodil moor and the downhill to Kentmere Hall. After about two kilometres the right of way continues onto a paved concourse through the heating and ventilating factory at Waterford Bridge.

4 Remain on the allocated section of the paving until you reach the barrier signifying the end of the factory, then turn right and follow the lane on the left signposted for Kentmere Pottery. When you reach the pottery at the end of the paved lane, take the unmarked path on the left which leads you between metal garden fences, over a small footbridge and through a pedestrian gate. After a further hundred metres or so, take a left onto the main outgoing path and return downhill to the start at Ulthwaite Bridge.

KENTMERE CHURCH ON THE DESCENT FROM THE DAFFODIL MOOR
(Roger Blamire)

Trail N4: Kentmere Reservoir

The reservoir is at the head of the Kentmere Valley and is just south of the source of the River Kent which passes through Staveley and Kendal on its way to the west coast between Arnside and Grange. The trail is easily navigable without a map and covers a range of surfaces, heading through small farms and past long-obsolete slate quarries on the edge of the valley floor.

Approximate Distance:	10.0 km/6.0 miles.
Terrain:	Road surfaces, grassy paths and gravel tracks.
Severity:	A straightforward run with deceptive elements of uphill on the route to the reservoir and generally easy running on the return.
Approximate Time:	45-65 minutes.
Total Ascent:	327m.
Start of the Trail:	From Staveley drive north on the Kentmere road for approximately four miles to reach the village. Bear west and park just beyond St Cuthbert's Church, next to the Village Institute. There is a courtesy box here, with a request for £3. During certain periods of the year, particularly in good weather, it may not be possible to find a parking space here and other options in the village may have to be considered. A local farmer often makes a field on the way into the village available for parking, again with a courtesy box.
Map Reference:	NY 456 041 (OS Explorer Map OL7: South-Eastern Lakes – North Sheet)

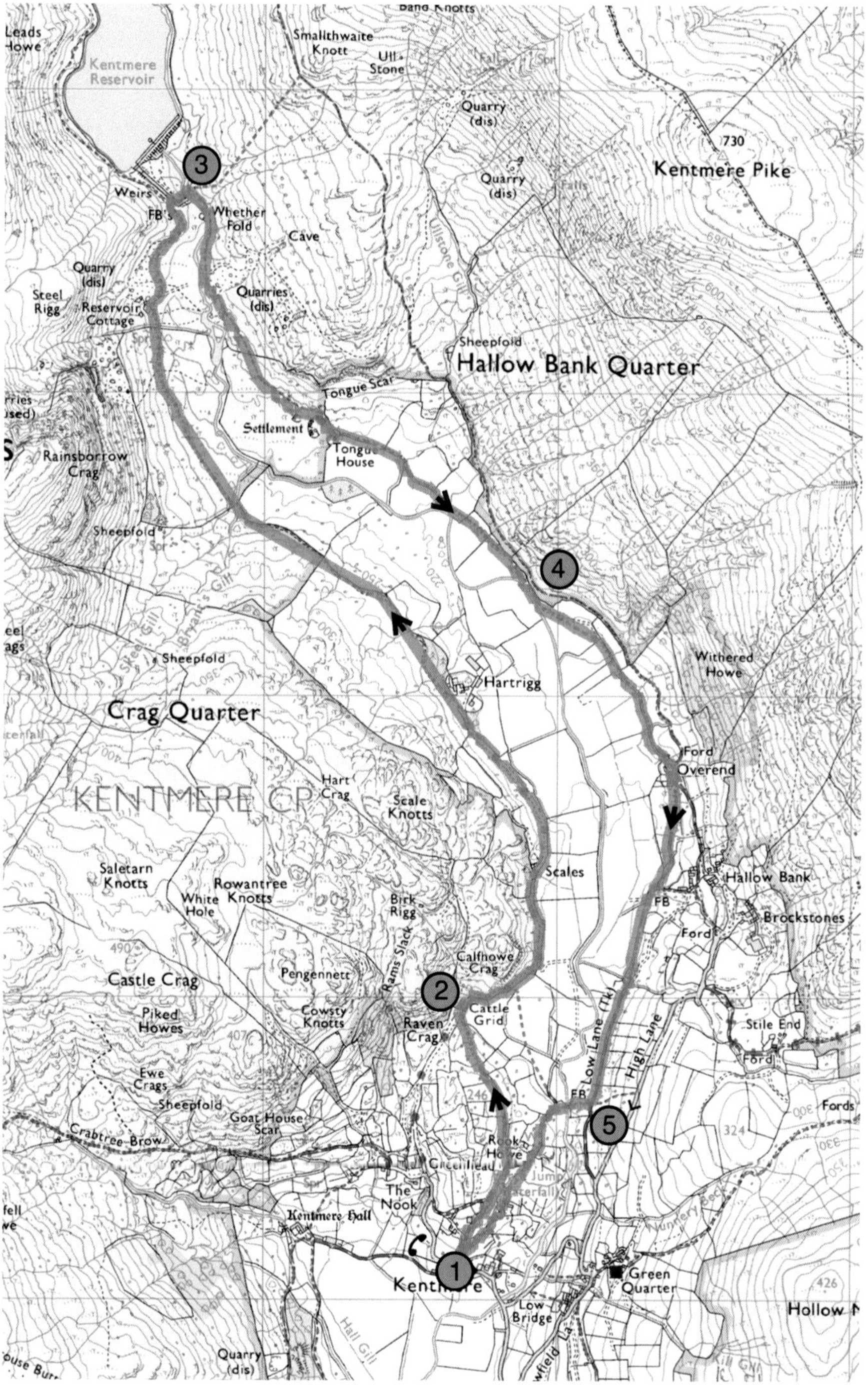
Kentmere Reservoir
Smallthwaite Knott
Ull Stone
Quarry (dis)
Kentmere Pike
3
Weirs
FB's
Whether Fold
Cave
Quarry (dis)
Steel Rigg
Reservoir Cottage
Quarries (dis)
Sheepfold
Hallow Bank Quarter
Tongue Scar
Settlement
Tongue House
Rainsborrow Crag
Sheepfold
4
Sheepfold
Hartrigg
Withered Howe
Crag Quarter
Ford
Overend
KENTMERE CP
Hart Crag
Scale Knotts
Scales
Hallow Bank
Saletarn Knotts
Rowantree Knotts
White Hole
Birk Rigg
FB
Brockstones
Ford
Castle Crag
Pengennett
Calfhowe Crag
2
Cattle Grid
Low Lane (Tk)
High Lane
Stile End
Piked Howes
Cowsty Knotts
Raven Crag
Ford
Ewe Crags
Sheepfold
FB
5
Fords
Goat House Scar
Crabtree Brow
Rook Howe
The Nook
Kentmere Hall
1
Kentmere
Green Quarter
Low Bridge
Hollow
Quarry (dis)
Hall Gill

1 Head north from the east side of the church on the steep uphill paved lane, which passes houses and through gates to reach a grassy path between field walls. After 400 metres you will come to a junction towards Rook Howe farm on the right. However, carry straight on up and over the incline, heading downhill to join the paved road north out of the village, at a cattle grid below Calfhowe Crag.

2 Turn right and continue on the road as it sweeps right then left past the crag, passing the converted barn at Scales on the left to reach Hartrigg Farm. Stay on the main path as the surface changes from paved to grass and gravel below Rainsborrow Crag. Shortly you will pass Reservoir Cottage, which is a bothy owned by Blackburn with Darwen Borough Council, for use by their Young People's Services. Just beyond the cottage the dam at the southern end of the reservoir comes into view.

3 Before reaching the dam the path turns to the right, taking you across a timber footbridge over the River Kent. Descend to the grassy and uneven path on the other side. The narrow path turns southwards and wends its way past some old slate quarries and an ancient British settlement to reach Tongue House. Skirt the house on the left and carry on, through field gates and past a packhorse bridge, following the Kent's route south.

4 The path shortly heads diagonally away from the river to reach the listed Overend Farm and farmhouse holiday cottages where it merges with the high-level path down from Nan Bield Pass. Look for a field gate with a waymark sign on the right at the far end of the buildings and follow this along a less distinct path, turning right then left after 400 metres. Continue onto the track between field walls, towards Green Quarter.

5 After a further 400 metres or so, look for the wall stiles on opposite sides of the track. Cross the stile on the right which leads you down to a timber footbridge over the Kent, up a short incline across a field, through a wall gap and onto an enclosed lane. Turn left here and continue on past Rook Howe, taking the left-hand footpath which carries on to meet the paved lane next to the church, leading you back to the car park.

HEADING TOWARDS CALFHOWE CRAG
(© Jumpy James)
www.jumpyjames.co.uk

Trail N5: Rydal Water and The Coffin Route

Although Rydal Water is within the northern boundary of the South Lakes it is quintessentially of Central Lakeland with its surrounding fells and pervasive tourism. This trail has historic references, including Rydal Mount, the home of William Wordsworth from 1813 until his death in 1850, which is an extremely popular tourist attraction. The Coffin Route refers to the path which was used for the bearing of coffins from Rydal to the cemetery at St Oswald's Church in Grasmere for burial.

The start of this trail is accessible by the 555 Stagecoach bus which travels between Kendal and Keswick.

Approximate Distance:	5.0 km/3.0 miles
Terrain:	Mostly reconstructed paths of slate and gravel, with a limited amount of road surface.
Severity:	Deceptively tough up and down running for the first half, over occasionally rocky paths. Some level or slightly downhill sections, particularly on the latter half of the run.
Approximate Time:	25-40 minutes
Total Ascent:	215m.
Start of the Trail:	Drive north on the A591 passing through Windermere and Ambleside. Shortly after leaving Ambleside you will reach the sign for Rydal. Look for the left-hand junction to Under Loughrigg, which takes you across the narrow Pelter Bridge. Turn right at the other side of the bridge and travel uphill for about 100 metres to the car park on the left. There is a charge for parking here.
Map Reference:	NY 364 060 (OS Explorer Map OL7: South-Eastern Lakes – North Sheet)

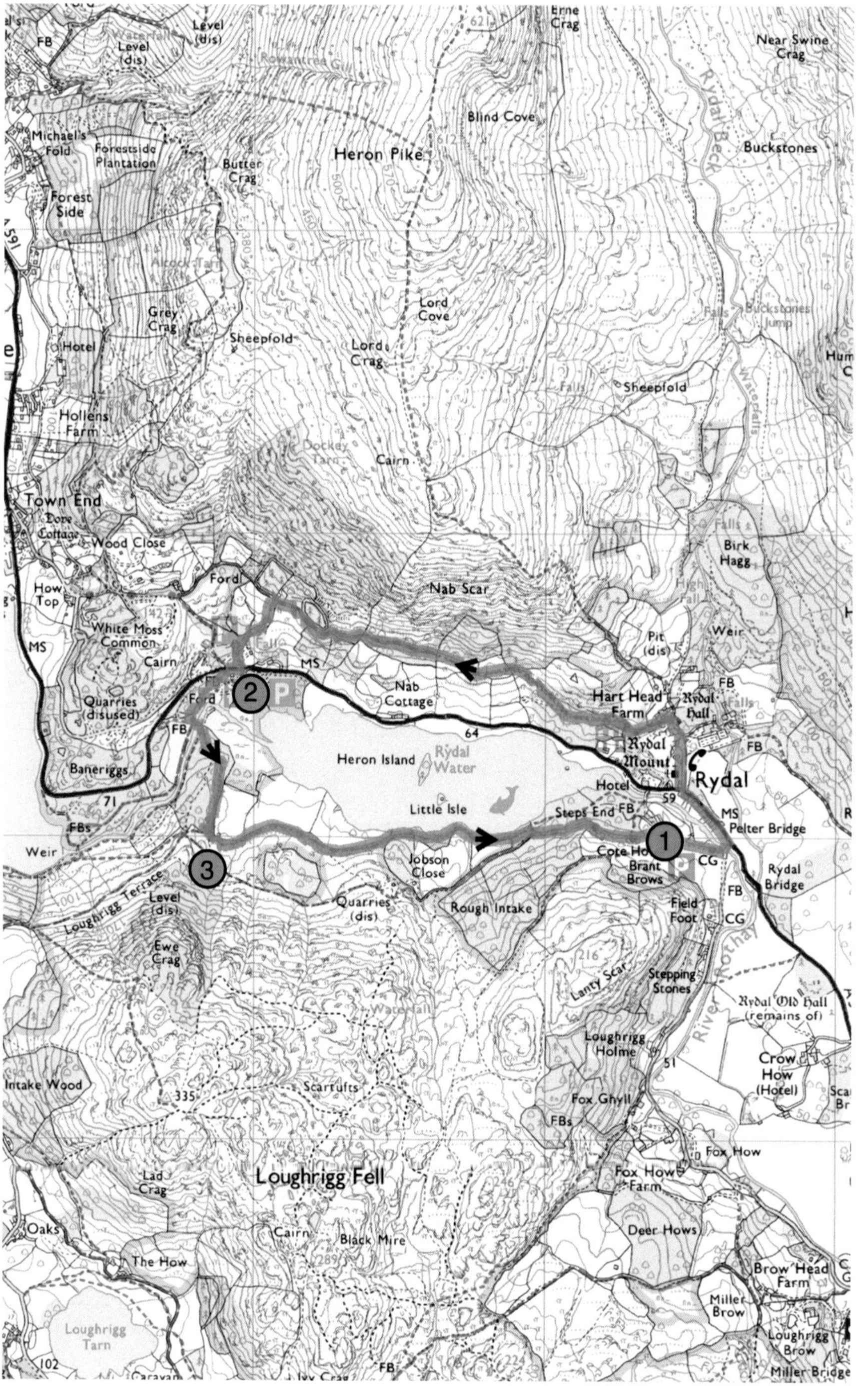
Level (dis)
Level (dis)
FB
Erne Crag
Near Swine Crag
Blind Cove
Heron Pike
Rydal Beck
Buckstones
Michael's Fold
Forestside Plantation
Butter Crag
Forest Side
A 591
Grey Crag
Lord Cove
Sheepfold
Lord Crag
Hotel
Buckstones Jump
Falls
Sheepfold
Hollens Farm
Cairn
Town End
Dove Cottage
Wood Close
Birk Hagg
Ford
Nab Scar
How Top
White Moss Common
Weir
Pit (dis)
MS
Cairn
MS
2
P
Nab Cottage
Hart Head Farm
Rydal Hall
FB
Quarries (disused)
Ford
FB
64
Rydal Mount
Rydal
Heron Island
Rydal Water
Baneriggs
Hotel
59
71
Little Isle
Steps End
FB
MS
Pelter Bridge
FBs
1
Weir
Cote How
Brant Brows
CG
3
Jobson Close
Rydal Bridge
Loughrigg Terrace
Level (dis)
Quarries (dis)
Rough Intake
FB
Field Foot
CG
Ewe Crag
216
Lanty Scar
Stepping Stones
River Rothay
Rydal Old Hall (remains of)
Loughrigg Holme
51
Crow How (Hotel)
Intake Wood
335
Scartufts
Fox Ghyll
FBs
Fox How
Lad Crag
Loughrigg Fell
Fox How Farm
Oaks
Cairn
Black Mire
Deer Hows
The How
289
Brow Head Farm
Miller Brow
Loughrigg Tarn
Loughrigg Brow
102
FB
Miller Bridge

1 Set out east from the car park and jog back down the lane and across the bridge to the A591 main road. Turn left and run along the pavement for about 200 metres until you see the signs for Rydal Hall and Rydal Mount on the right-hand side of the road. Carefully cross the busy road and head uphill on the steep lane, past the entrances to Rydal Hall and Rydal Mount. Following a particularly steep section on concrete at the top of the lane, look for the sign for The Coffin Route on the left-hand side. Follow the path through the gate which fronts a narrow lane and emerges onto the route itself.

Continue on the undulating path, passing through several gates. After about one kilometre you will encounter a particularly rocky section adjacent to a wall on your left. Shortly after that, you will come to a junction, with a rendered dwelling house on the right-hand side, above the path. The main path continues on to Grasmere but take the left-hand path down a steep incline and through a further gate until you reach the A591 at White Moss.

2 Carefully cross the road and run past the slate-built toilets and across a small footbridge on your right. Continue on to the smooth gravel track along the side of the River Rothay, which floods onto the path from time to time. Shortly you will reach a modern metal footbridge which you should cross, taking the track directly ahead of you, signposted for 'Rydal Caves'. Run through the woodland and the long uphill to a gate in a stone wall.

3 Run on for a few metres and take the path to the left and downhill to the water side. Continue on this path until you reach a junction near the end of the lake. Stay on the main route which takes you uphill to a gate and signpost for Ambleside. The path soon becomes a paved country lane passing some houses on both sides of the road, including the wedding venue at Cote Howe. Carry on downhill and back to the car park.

HEADING ALONG THE COFFIN ROUTE FROM RYDAL MOUNT
(© Jumpy James)
www.jumpyjames.co.uk

Trail N6: Sadgill to Green Quarter

Longsleddale is an isolated, sparsely populated valley of sheep farms and pasture, which is immediately east of the Kentmere Valley. It is dissected by the River Sprint which travels north to south to meet the River Kent at Burneside.

The trail sets out from Sadgill which is at the northern end of the paved road up the valley. It takes in the reverse direction of the initial ascent of the Kentmere Horseshoe from Kentmere Village, to the base of the path up Shipman's Knott.

There are two alternative options to this trail, which are described as addenda.

Approximate Distance:	9.5 km/6.0 miles
Terrain:	Tracks, road and grassy paths
Severity:	Steep uphill to the head of the pass and a shorter downhill on the farm track on the return to Sadgill. Less severe ascents and descents on the grassy paths round Green Quarter and Cocklaw Fells.
Approximate Time:	50-70 minutes
Total Ascent:	427m.
Start of the Trail:	Head north out of Kendal on the A6 towards Shap. In approximately four miles you will see the junction to Longsleddale on the left. Take this narrow country road downhill, passing through the pleasant hamlet of Garnett Bridge after quarter of a mile. Head north on the road signposted for Longsleddale, following the River Sprint in reverse up the valley. After three miles you will come to St Mary's Church on the left-hand side of the road. Continue on for a further two and a half miles until the paved surface ends at the bridge over the Sprint at Sadgill, where there is usually plenty of parking space.
Map Reference:	NY 483 058 (OS Explorer Map OL7: South-Eastern Lakes – North Sheet)

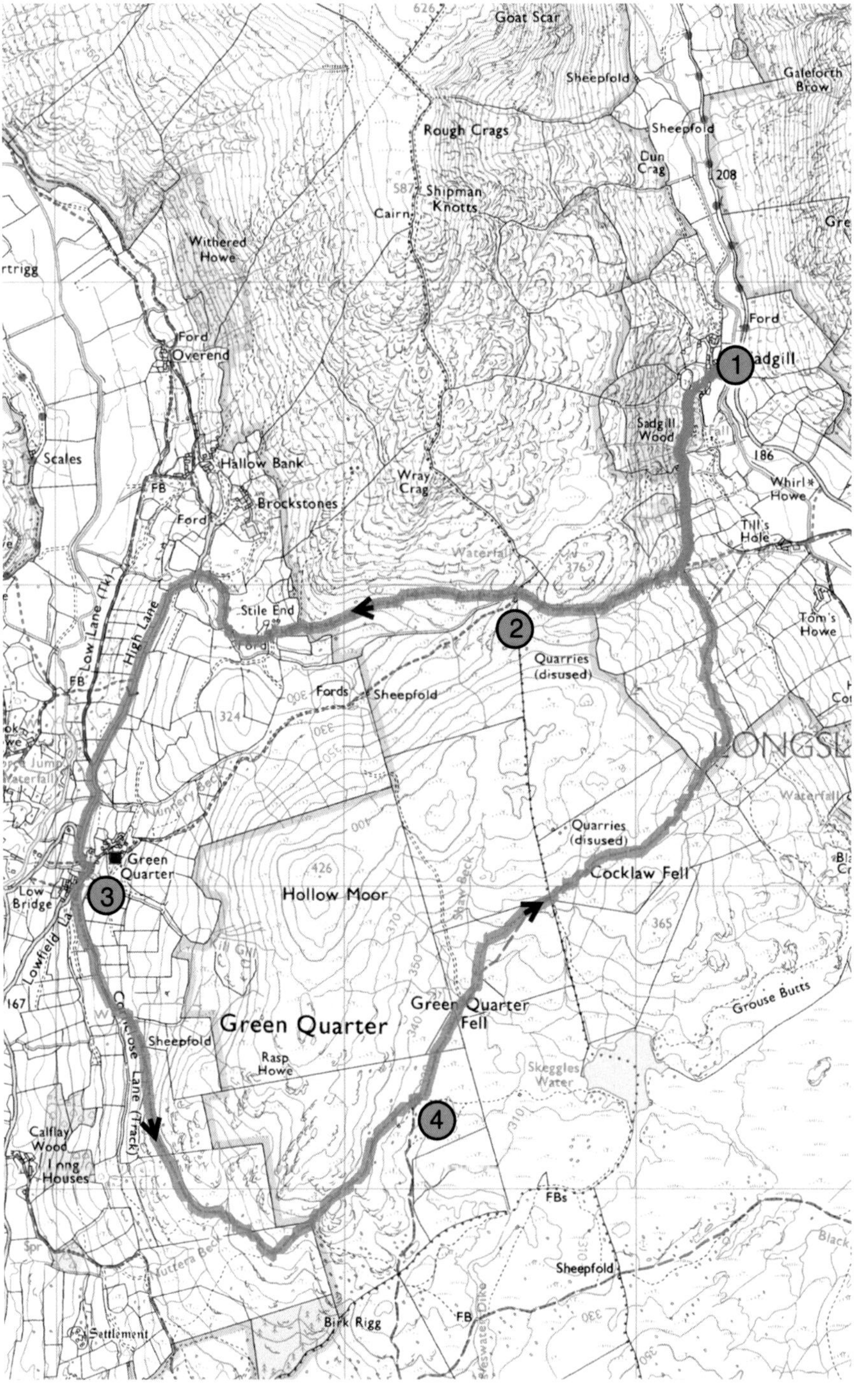
Goat Scar
Sheepfold
Galeforth Brow
Rough Crags
Sheepfold
Dun Crag
208
Shipman Knotts
587
Cairn
Withered Howe
Ford
Overend
Ford
1
Sadgill
Sadgill Wood
186
Whirl Howe
Scales
Hallow Bank
FB
Brockstones
Ford
Wray Crag
Till's Hole
Waterfall
376
Stile End
Ford
2
Quarries (disused)
Tom's Howe
Low Lane (Tk)
High Lane
FB
Fords
Sheepfold
324
Quarries (disused)
Green Quarter
Low Bridge
3
Hollow Moor
426
Cocklaw Fell
365
Lowfield La
167
Green Quarter Fell
Grouse Butts
Green Quarter
Sheepfold
Rasp Howe
Skeggles Water
4
Calflay Wood
Long Houses
FBs
Sheepfold
Settlement
Birk Rigg
FB

1 Set out across the bridge over the Sprint at Sadgill and follow the farm track as it heads left and then right and left again, ascending the steep incline on the rocky, occasionally reconstructed, path through a gate (where the path meets the return route from Cocklaw Fell) and on to the top of the pass at the base of Shipman's Knott.

2 Stay on the main bridleway as it descends to Stile End and onto the paved surface of High Lane at the bottom of the hill. Turn left at the lane and continue downhill, ignoring the junction to the right, and carry on, bearing left towards Green Quarter.

3 Turn right at the road junction below Green Quarter and head south for a short distance to a field gate and sign for Cocklaw Fell and Longsleddale on the left. Follow the clear, grassy path uphill taking a left at a junction and continuing onto the open moorland between Green Quarter and Cocklaw Fells.

4 Pass derelict shepherd's cottages and the junction with the path up from Haw Lane as you go. On the descent you will see Skeggles Water in the near distance to the right. Continue to loop the fell and head down to meet the gate and bridleway up from Sadgill. Turn right and return downhill to the start.

ADDENDUM A

Follow the bridleway and lane to Green Quarter as described in 1 and 2 above. At Green Quarter, pass the junction with the road south and head uphill past Maggs Howe Bed and Breakfast establishment, and between camping barns. You will reach footpath signage which directs you onto a grassy path uphill and across fields and open moorland, to reach the top of the pass below Shipman's Knott. Pass through the gate, turn right and return down the rocky bridleway to Sadgill.

(8.0 km/5.0 miles)

ADDENDUM B

Follow the bridleway as described in 1 above. At the head of the pass turn left off the bridleway and onto the reverse direction of the grassy path across moorland to reach the paved surface at Green Quarter. Head down to the junction with the road south, turn left and follow the sign for the path round the fells as described in 3 and 4 above.

(9.5km/6.0 miles)

DESCENDING INTO GREEN QUARTER FROM SADGILL (Addendum B)
(The Author)

Trail N7: Alcock Tarn

This trail, which is located adjacent to Trails N1 and N5, combines magnificent scenery as well as the severity of a short Category A fell race. However, it comes with a 'Health Warning'. The ascent and descent, while affording wonderful views of Grasmere and the surrounding fells, are very steep and rocky in places and great care should be taken to avoid trips and ankle injuries, particularly on the descent from the tarn.

The tarn and lower reaches are within land owned by the National Trust.

The start of this trail is accessible by the 555 Stagecoach bus which travels between Kendal and Keswick.

Approximate Distance:	7.5 km/4.75 miles.
Terrain:	Road surfaces and a well-constructed, mostly gravel and occasionally rocky path on the ascent to the tarn. The path on the descent is very rocky for long sections, especially at the top, and does require extreme care to avoid falls or damage to legs and ankles.
Severity:	Very steep climb to the tarn, with equally steep descent on the north side. Occasional inclines on the road back from the roundabout next to the Wordsworth Centre.
Approximate Time:	45-70 minutes.
Total Ascent:	446m.
Start of the Trail:	From Ambleside, drive north on the A591 passing Rydal Water until you see White Moss car park on the left. Carry on for a short distance and turn right into the pay car park on the other side of the road.
Map Reference:	NY 348 066 (OS Explorer Map OL7: South-Eastern Lakes – North Sheet)

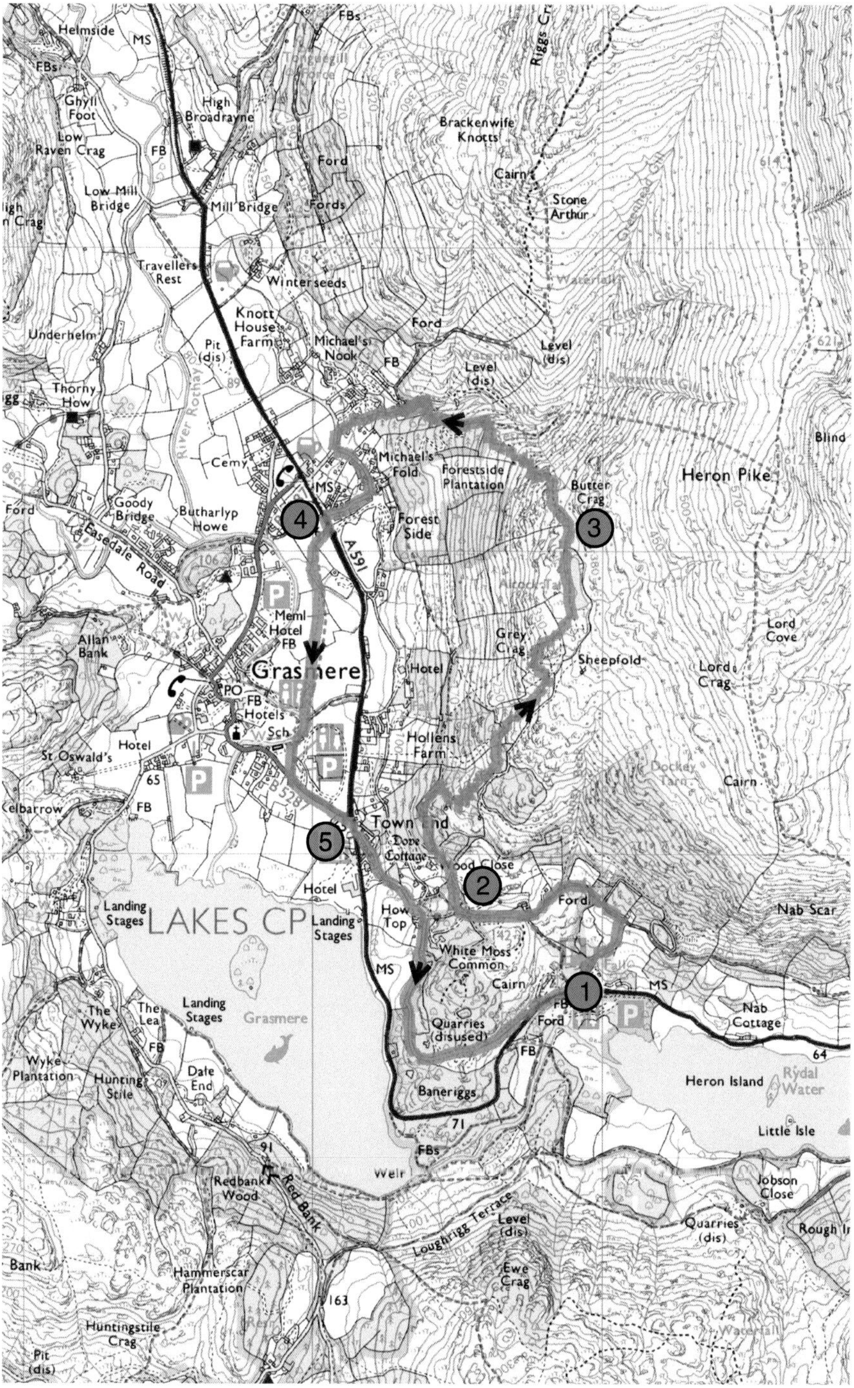
1
2
3
4
5
Helmside
MS
FBs
Ghyll Foot
High Broadrayne
Low Raven Crag
FB
Ford
Low Mill Bridge
Mill Bridge
Fords
Brackenwife Knotts
Cairn
Stone Arthur
Travellers Rest
Winterseeds
Knott House Farm
Underhelm
Pit (dis)
Michael's Nook
Ford
FB
Level (dis)
Thorny How
Cemy
Michael's Fold
Forestside Plantation
Butter Crag
Heron Pike
Blind
Goody Bridge
Butharlyp Howe
Forest Side
Easedale Road
A591
Meml Hotel
FB
Allan Bank
Grey Crag
Sheepfold
Lord Cove
Grasmere
Hotel
Lord Crag
PO
FB
Hotels
Sch
Hollens Farm
Hotel
St Oswald's
65
Cairn
Town End
Dove Cottage
Wood Close
FB
Hotel
Ford
Landing Stages
LAKES CP
How Top
Nab Scar
White Moss Common
Cairn
MS
MS
The Wyke
The Lea
Landing Stages
Grasmere
Quarries (disused)
FB
Ford
Nab Cottage
64
Wyke Plantation
Hunting Stile
Dale End
Baneriggs
Heron Island
Rydal Water
71
Little Isle
91
FBs
Weir
Redbank Wood
Red Bank
Jobson Close
Loughrigg Terrace
Level (dis)
Quarries (dis)
Rough
Bank
Hammerscar Plantation
Ewe Crag
163
Huntingstile Crag
Pit (dis)

1 From the car park head back towards Rydal, on the same side of the road, for a few metres and look for the path on the left. Take this steep uphill passing through a metal gate to reach the Coffin Route (see Trail N5). Take a left at the junction, where a house is located, and follow the pleasant, level path round past the gully at Dunney Beck.

Shortly you will pass the signposted junction with another path up from the car park. Continue on the main path for 250 metres, looking for a track on the right, signposted for 'Alcock Tarn 1¼ miles'.

2 Follow this rocky but easily negotiable track for a short distance, to reach a field gate for Brackenfell National Trust land where you will see a sign for Alcock Tarn. Do not be tempted to take the path uphill to the right at this point but go through the gate into woods, continuing uphill to reach a second National Trust gate onto the open fell.

At a junction take the yellow waymark to the right (ignoring the white one to the left) and continue winding uphill on the steep incline. At the top of this arduous climb[7] you will reach a grassy plateau where the path bears to the left and heads through a wall gap to reach the tarn. Carry on along the left-hand (west) side of the tarn.

3 The path becomes very rocky as you start to descend away from the tarn and this continues for some distance as you zigzag cautiously downhill. At this point there are panoramic views of Grasmere and the surrounding fells, including 'The Lion and the Lamb' on Helm Crag, and you will feel a wonderful sense of space as you look over the gully to Stone Arthur to the north. From here, descend towards the fir plantation, bearing to the right and continuing down adjacent to a wall on your left, at the edge of the plantation.

When you reach an inaccessible gate into the plantation, the path heads to the right and across a footbridge over Rowantree Gill. The gravel path on the other side leads you left and down to a gate, and onto a paved lane serving a number of private homes. The lane soon reaches a minor road, where you head left and down to main A591 road. Alternatively, you can bear left at the first junction and follow the lane between more well-appointed houses, before descending to the main road.

4 Turn left and cross the road to the pavement on the other side, and go right after a short distance following the line of the footpath sign which directs you diagonally left, and cross the fields and meadow to the gate in the corner. Pass the footbridge over the River Rothay at this point and continue straight on, alongside the car park to reach Stock Lane into Grasmere Village. Turn left here, heading away from the village, and continue for 250 metres to reconnect with the A591 at the roundabout, where the Wordsworth Museum is located.

5 Take a left off the A591 and onto the minor road signposted for Dove Cottage. Continue on this lane, up a long ascent and along a 'switch back' leading you, after a further kilometre, back to the car park and the start of the run.

LOOKING BACK TOWARDS LAKE WINDERMERE FROM ALCOCK TARN
(© Jumpy James)
www.jumpyjames.co.uk

[7] The tarn is at an altitude of 370 metres, compared with 170 metres at the base of the climb.

THE WEST

Trail W1: Great Langdale Valley

This trail takes in the iconic valley of Great Langdale, which provides access to many of the principal fells of Lakeland including the Langdale Pikes, Pike o' Blisco, the Crinkle Crags and Bow Fell, with routes through to Great Gable and Scafell Pike.

It sets out from the pretty villages of Elterwater and Chapel Stile at the eastern end of the valley, and takes in sections of the Cumbria Way which covers 70 miles between Ulverston and Carlisle.

Approximate Distance:	10.0 km/6.0 miles
Terrain:	Paved surfaces and well-constructed, mostly gravel, paths on the outward section. The path on the return journey is more typical of a low level fell run, with reconstructed surfaces and grassy paths leading to paved lanes as it arrives back at the Elterwater area.
Severity:	Mostly level on the outward section along the valley floor, with much more undulating terrain on the return.
Approximate Time:	50-70 minutes.
Total Ascent:	231m.
Start of the Trail:	From Ambleside, drive west on the A593 past Clappersgate, following the course of the River Brathay to reach Skelwith Bridge. At the hotel, take the right-hand fork onto the B5343 towards Great Langdale. After a further mile and a half you will come to a branch off to the left which takes you into Elterwater village. Drive past the Britannia Inn on the right and park at the public pay car park on the left, just before the bridge over Great Langdale Beck.
Map Reference:	NY 328 047 (OS Explorer Map OL7: South-Eastern Area – North Sheet) (The trail continues onto OS Explorer Map OL6: South-Western Area – North Sheet for a short distance at the western end of the loop).

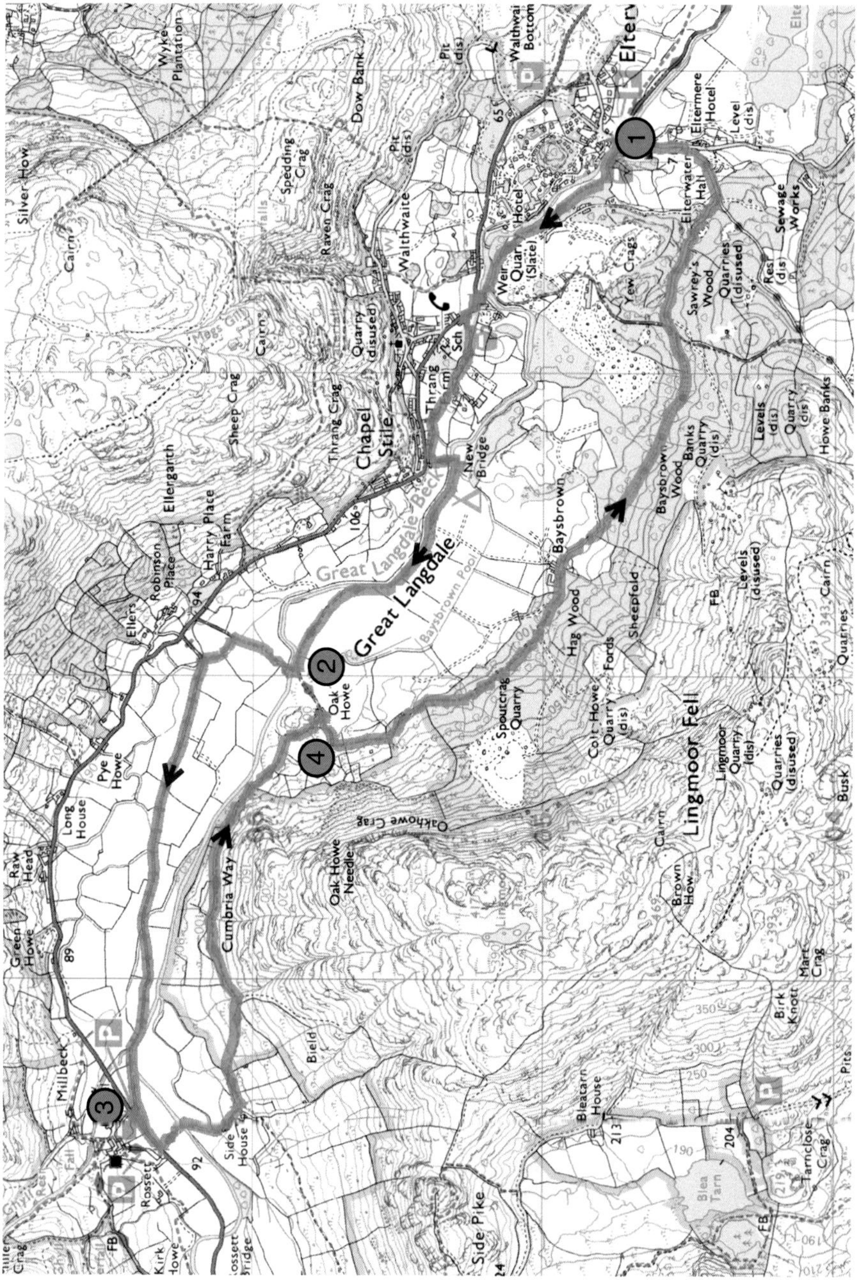
1
2
3
4
Great Langdale
Great Langdale Beck
Chapel Stile
Lingmoor Fell
Cumbria Way
Silver How
Wyke Plantation
Dow Bank
Spedding Crag
Raven Crag
Walthwaite
Thrang Crag
Sheep Crag
Ellergarth
Harry Place Farm
Robinson Place
Ellers
Pye Howe
Long House
Raw Head
Green Howe
Millbeck
Rossett
Side House
Side Pike
Bield
Oak Howe
Oak Howe Needle
Oakhowe Crag
New Bridge
Baysbrown
Baysbrown Pool
Baysbrown Wood
Hag Wood
Sheepfold
Spoutcrag Quarry
Colt Howe Quarry (dis)
Fords
Brown How
Blea Tarn
Bleatarn House
Tarnclose Crag
Birk Knott
Mart Crag
Busk
Howe Banks
Sawrey's Wood
Yew Crags
Weir Quarry (Slate)
Elterwater Hall
Elterwater Hotel
Sewage Works
Walthwaite Bottom

1 From the car park cross the road bridge over Great Langdale Beck and turn right on the paved surface, heading uphill alongside the river. At the top of the incline, turn right at the signpost, off the lane and onto a gravel path heading downhill. Take extra care on the short section of reconstructed path alongside the river edge. As the main path turns to the left, cross the pedestrian bridge ahead and pass through a gate to emerge onto the road between Elterwater and Chapel Stile.

Turn left onto the road, passing Wainwright's Inn, and, after a further few metres, turn left again and onto a gravel footpath signposted for Great Langdale. Head for the sign at Thrang Farm and skirt the farm on the right. The path passes an obsolete slate quarry, turning left and crossing a footbridge, and then right, along a paved path beside Baysbrown Campsite. Follow the winding trail alongside Great Langdale Beck for 800 metres until you come to a junction of paths.

2 Take the right-hand path across another footbridge and continue over a field to a gate. The main footpath turns left here and continues on as a byway, heading diagonally across the fields to re-join the banks of the beck. Cross the bridge to reach the B5343 next to the New Dungeon Ghyll Hotel, at the base of the main path up to Stickle Tarn and the Langdale Pikes.

3 Continue along the road and look for the signposted path on the left after 100 metres. Cross the field and another footbridge over the beck to reach Side House Farm. Look for the waymarked sign on the left through a gate and follow the reconstructed path on a steep uphill away from the farm, on the route of the Cumbria Way. The uneven fellside path follows a wall and skirts the fell on the right to reach the converted holiday cottage at Oak Howe.

4 Turn right here onto a gravel path which loops round to the right and then left through the woodland at the base of Lingmoor Fell, to reach Baysbrown Farm. Pass through the farmyard and onto the paved access lane through more woodland. Ignore the offshoot to the left, which takes you through to the outgoing path near Wainwright's Inn, and continue through the woods on the paved surface. You will see the busy workings of the Elterwater Quarry, which produces Burlington Slate, through the trees on the left.

The lane passes the junction with a path through to Little Langdale on the right to reach the road junction at Eltermere Hotel, just beyond Eltermere Hall. Turn left onto the main road and continue downhill for 250 metres to the bridge at the starting point.

THE LANGDALE PIKES FROM SIDE HOUSE FARM
(The Author)

Trail W2: Bigland Tarn

This trail starts near Haverthwaite where the steam railway sets out on the return journey of the 3.2 mile heritage line from Lakeside, at the southern tip of Lake Windermere. The trail passes some pretty hamlets, and Bigland Tarn, and takes in parts of the Cumbria Coastal Way, which covers 182 miles between Silverdale in Lancashire and Gretna in Dumfries and Galloway.

Approximate Distance:	8.5 km/5.25 miles
Terrain:	Mostly stony paths and road surfaces.
Severity:	Long climb to Bigland Tarn at the beginning but thereafter relatively easy going.
Approximate Time:	40-60 minutes.
Total Ascent:	314m.
Start of the Trail:	From Plumgarth Roundabout head south on the A591 dual carriageway, bypassing Kendal. Come off at the signage for Barrow and travel west on the A590. In just over fifteen miles, after passing Newby Bridge and Backbarrow, take the B5278 road signposted for Haverthwaite and Holker Hall on the left-hand side of the main road. Turn sharp left on this road after half a mile, following the sign for Holker Hall, cross the River Leven and park in the layby on the right-hand side of the Cark road, just after the sign to Low Wood.
Map Reference:	SD 346 835 (OS Explorer Map OL7: South-Eastern Lakes – South Sheet)

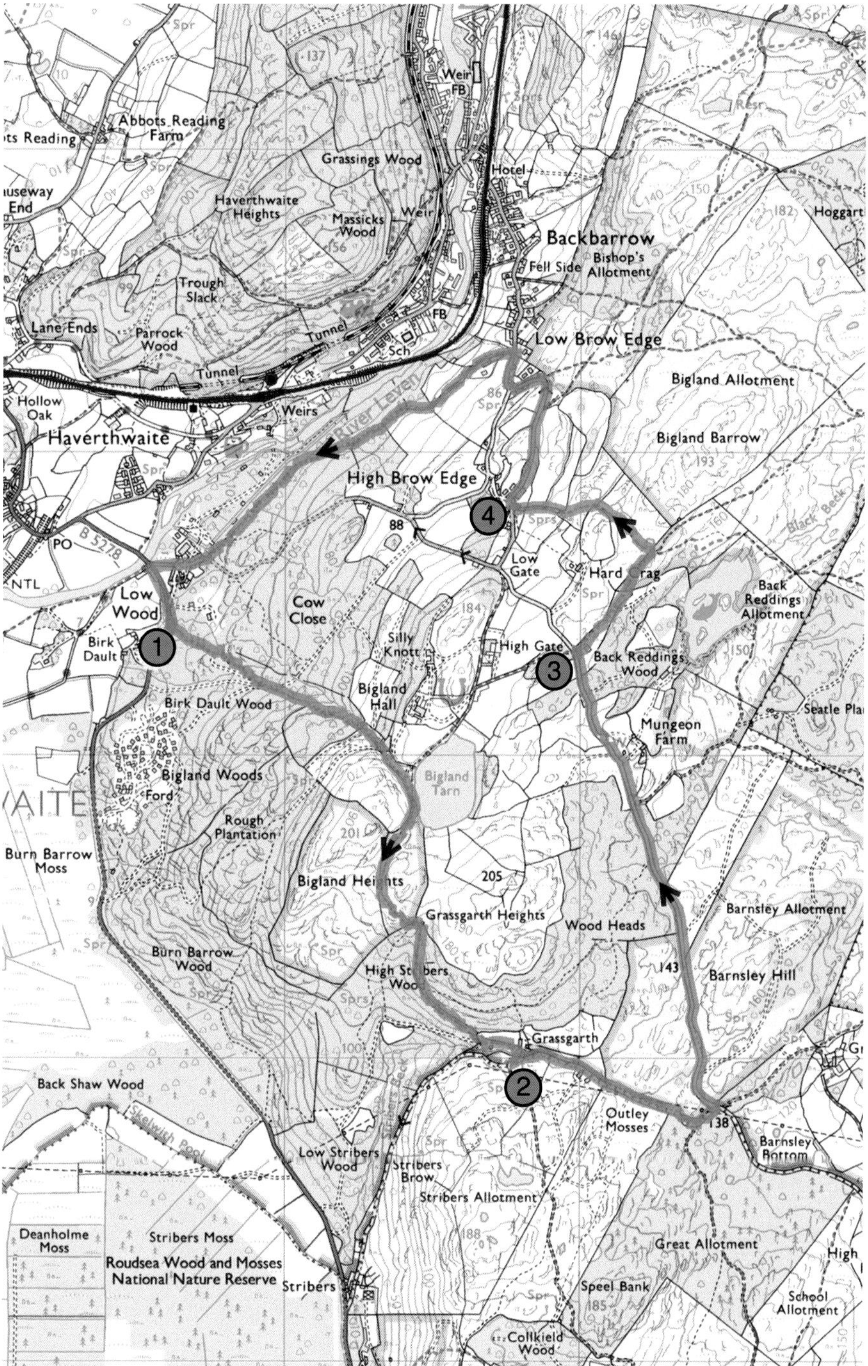

Abbots Reading Farm
Grassings Wood
Haverthwaite Heights
Massicks Wood
Backbarrow
Bishop's Allotment
Fell Side
Trough Slack
Lane Ends
Parrock Wood
Low Brow Edge
Bigland Allotment
Hollow Oak
Haverthwaite
Weirs
River Leven
Bigland Barrow
High Brow Edge
Low Gate
Hard Crag
Low Wood
Cow Close
Back Reddings Allotment
Birk Dault
Silly Knott
High Gate
Back Reddings Wood
Bigland Hall
Birk Dault Wood
Mungeon Farm
Seatle
Bigland Woods
Bigland Tarn
Ford
Rough Plantation
Burn Barrow Moss
Bigland Heights
Grassgarth Heights
Wood Heads
Barnsley Allotment
Burn Barrow Wood
High Stribers Wood
Barnsley Hill
Grassgarth
Back Shaw Wood
Outley Mosses
Skelwith Pool
Low Stribers Wood
Stribers Brow
Barnsley Bottom
Stribers Allotment
Deanholme Moss
Stribers Moss
Great Allotment
Roudsea Wood and Mosses National Nature Reserve
Stribers
Speel Bank
School Allotment
Colkield Wood
Hotel
Weir
FB
Tunnel
Sch
PO
NTL
B 5278
1
2
3
4

1 Jog back on the road for 50 metres and take the signposted path on the right, onto the Cumbria Coastal Way. Head up the steep path, through dense woodland for 1200 metres, to reach open grassland at the top. Bear right on the path alongside Bigland Tarn, following the yellow waymarks.

There is a magnificent, panoramic view of the River Leven estuary as you head downhill and through a gate into High Scribbers Wood. Continue downhill through the wood, emerging into fields at the bottom to reach the farm at Grassgarth. Cross a small footbridge on the right and head up and through the gate onto a paved lane.

2 Turn left at this point and head along the lane, taking a left at the junction after 400 metres, next to the entrance to Greenhurst House. Continue on this lane for a furthert 1200 metres, ignoring the first footpath sign on the right.

3 Look for a second sign at High Gate, opposite the gates to Bigland Hall and turn right onto the footpath through a field gate and onto a slated track. Cross a stone stile on the left after 400 metres and follow the directions of the sign for High Brow Edge, passing a small tarn and carrying on downhill past gorse bushes. Head slightly left to another stile in the corner of the field. Continue down and left to reach an enclosed path that leads you to High Brow Edge.

4 Pass through the field gate at High Brow Edge and onto the road, turning right. Ignore the junction to the left, and continue downhill towards Low Brow Edge. After two sweeping bends in the road, take the public bridleway on the left, signposted for Trundle Brow. Run downhill through the woods to a clearing and onto the road at Low Wood. Turn right and then left past stone terraced houses to join the Cark road. Turn left and head back along the short distance up to the layby.

LOOKING DOWN TOWARDS HIGH BROW EDGE
(The Author)

Trail W3: Hawkshead Forestry Loop

Hawkshead is a pretty tourist village of alleyways, overhanging gables and medieval squares at the northern end of Esthwaite Water, to the west of Lake Windermere.

The village has many historical references since it was originally owned by the monks of Furness Abbey, growing to be an important wool market in medieval times and later a market town. The poet William Wordsworth was educated at Hawkshead Grammar School in the late 18th century. Beatrix Potter owned Hill Top Farm at nearby Near Sawrey, where she spent many holidays away from London between 1905 and her death in 1943.

Much of the land in and around the village is now owned by the National Trust and the trail takes in the north east corner of the Grizedale Forest Park with its network of off-road cycling and mountain biking routes.

The start of the trail is accessible by the 505 Stagecoach bus from Ambleside.

Approximate Distance:	6.0 km/3.75 miles.
Terrain:	A combination of rocky and grassy footpaths, and forestry tracks, with a short section on road.
Severity:	Long uphill on a stony but clear path at the beginning, levelling out through the Forest Park, and downhill through meadow towards Esthwaite Water in the latter half of the run.
Approximate Time:	30-45 minutes.
Total Ascent:	221m.
Start of the Trail:	Hawkshead is accessible by way of the ferry service from Bowness-on-Windermere. Follow the B5285 road from the ferry through Far Sawrey and Near Sawrey for four miles and park in the main pay car park as you enter Hawkshead village from the south east. The alternative is to drive west from Ambleside to Clappersgate and then take the B5286, at the left-hand fork signposted for Hawkshead, following the signage to reach the village in approximately five miles.
Map Reference:	SD 353 981 (OS Explorer Map OL7: South-Eastern Lakes – North Sheet)

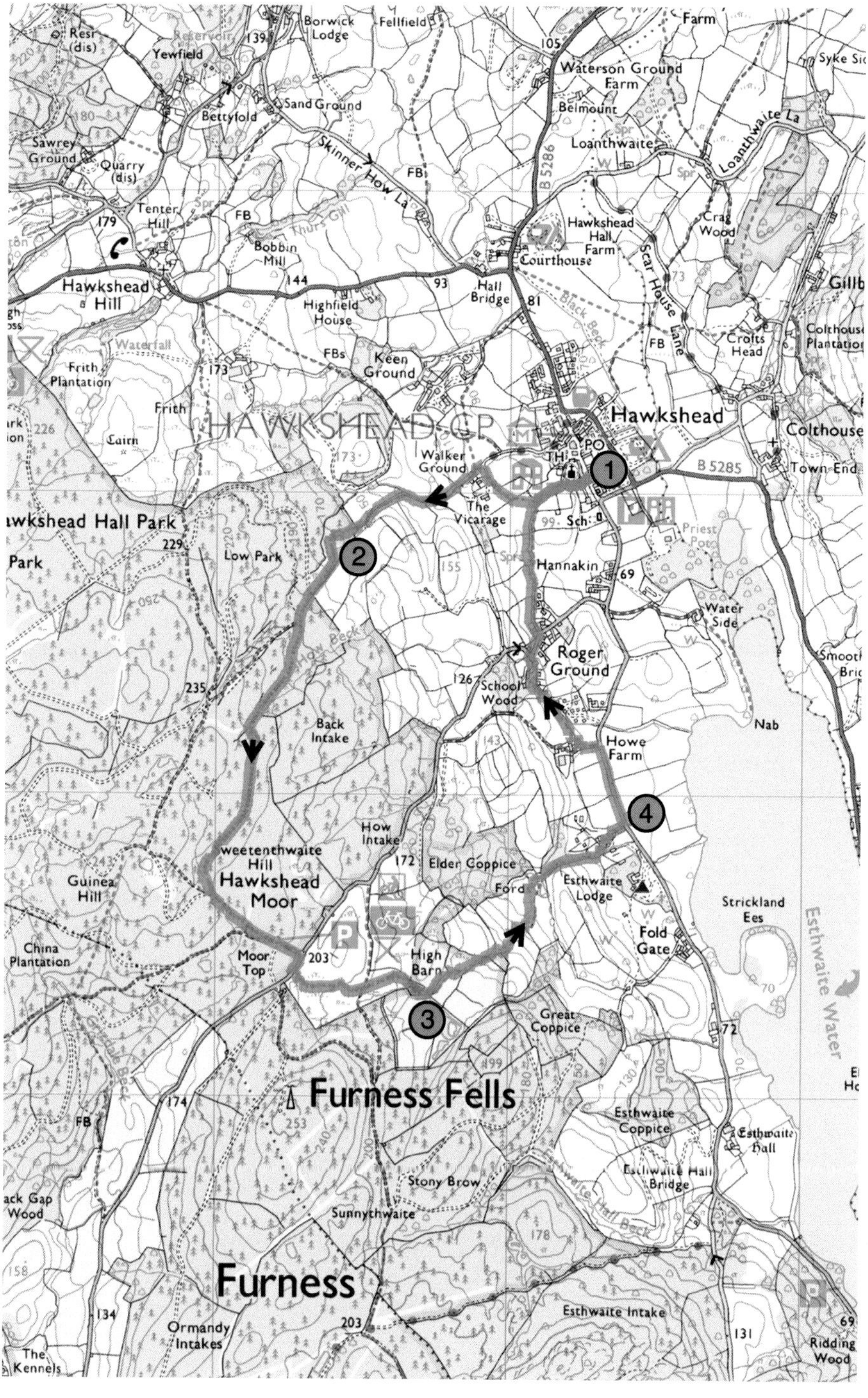
Resr (dis)
Borwick Lodge
Fellfield
Farm
Yewfield
Waterson Ground Farm
Sand Ground
Belmount
Bettyfold
Sawrey Ground
Quarry (dis)
Skinner How La
Loanthwaite
Loanthwaite La
FB
Tenter Hill
Hawkshead Hall Farm
Crag Wood
Bobbin Mill
Courthouse
Scar House Lane
Hawkshead Hill
Highfield House
Hall Bridge
Black Beck
Gillb
Frith Plantation
FBs
Keen Ground
Crofts Head
Colthouse Plantation
Frith
Hawkshead
Cairn
HAWKSHEAD CP
PO
TH
Colthouse
Walker Ground
B 5285
Town End
Hawkshead Hall Park
The Vicarage
Sch
Priest Pot
Low Park
Hannakin
Park
Water Side
Roger Ground
School Wood
Smooth Bri
Back Intake
Howe Farm
Nab
How Intake
Elder Coppice
weetenthwaite Hill
Hawkshead Moor
Guinea Hill
Esthwaite Lodge
Ford
Strickland Ees
China Plantation
Moor Top
High Barn
Fold Gate
Esthwaite Water
Great Coppice
Furness Fells
Esthwaite Coppice
Esthwaite Hall
Esthwaite Hall Bridge
Stony Brow
ack Gap Wood
Sunnythwaite
Esthwaite Hall Beck
Furness
Esthwaite Intake
Ormandy Intakes
Ridding Wood
The Kennels
1
2
3
4

1 Set out west from the car park and along the paved lane past Hawkshead Grammar School (now a museum). Go through the gate into the south side of the churchyard of St Michael's and run uphill past the graveyard to a gate in the top left-hand corner. Once through the gate, cross the next field, staying on the right-hand side next to the slated boundary stones, to a gate and signpost. The path to the left is signed for Roger Ground but go diagonally right for Vicarage Lane and Walker Ground, passing through a gate and along a path to the lane.

Turn left here onto a stone track and head uphill with a beck on your left. This is a long waymarked climb of about 800 metres, which bears left and crosses the beck before reaching a wide forestry track forming part of the network of cycling tracks within Grizedale Forest.

2 Go left here and continue up and over the high point of the track and down to the pay car park at Moor Top, ignoring the various offshoots (mostly for cyclists) to right and left. When you reach the road beyond the car park, go right for a few metres and then take the footpath on the left, signposted for High Barn and Esthwaite Water. Head downhill on the farm track to reach High Barn, enjoying the dramatic views of distant fells and Esthwaite Water in the near distance as you descend.

3 Pass through the field gate at High Barn and follow the path as it skirts the left-hand edge of the next field and bears right, through gates, across fields, and down to a beck with a small timber footbridge. Cross the bridge and go through the gate into woodland with the beck on your left, and head down the wide path to the pretty settlement of holiday cottages next to Esthwaite Lodge, to reach the road into Hawkeshead.

4 Turn left and run cautiously along the road for 250 metres to reach the path leading to Howe Farm on the left. Go up the path and turn right at the signage just before the farm buildings. Skirt the cottage garden and head into a field, staying on the right-hand side until you reach Roger Ground within a short distance. Continue on the paved surface between houses until you reach a bend in the road you crossed at Moor Top, next to a red post box.

Turn right and head down this road for 50 metres until you reach the lane taking you past Claife View on the left. The footpath sign here is slightly obscured. This lane takes you onto an enclosed path through gates and across pasture until you reach the sign for Roger Ground/Vicarage Lane which you encountered on the outward journey. Turn right here, go through the gates, and retrace your steps past the Church and the Grammar School and back to the car park.

THE SETTLEMENT OF HOLIDAY COTTAGES NEXT TO ESTHWAITE LODGE
(The Author)

Trail W4: The Hodge Close Round

This trail sets out from the dramatic Hodge Close Quarry, a massive excavation of light green coloured slate near Coniston. It negotiates a full circuit round the lower reaches of Holme Fell. The tarns below the fell are in fact reservoirs created to supply water to the adjacent quarry. From the nineteenth century until as recently as 1960 a gravity lifting device was used to raise blocks of slate from the 50-metre-deep quarry, using a tank, supplied with water from the tarns, as a counterbalance. The quarry is now popular with abseilers and divers.

A short section of the route is on the Cumbria Way which covers 70 miles between Ulverston and Carlisle.

Approximate Distance:	10.0 km/6.0 miles.
Terrain:	Paths and minor sections of road.
Severity:	Long sections of steady ascent and descent.
Approximate Time:	50-70 minutes.
Total Ascent:	400m.
Start of the Trail:	Take the A593 road west from Ambleside, passing through Clappersgate and turn left at Skelwith Bridge, heading towards Coniston. In approximately 4 miles, shortly after passing the National Trust car park at Glen Mary Bridge, look for the narrow country lane signposted 'Hodge Close Only' which meets the main road on the right-hand side, at Great Intake. Carry on northwards on the lane for one and a half miles until you reach the parking area at the quarry, which is cordoned off with large blocks of slate.
Map Reference:	NY 316 017 (OS Explorer Map OL7: South-Eastern Lakes- North Sheet)

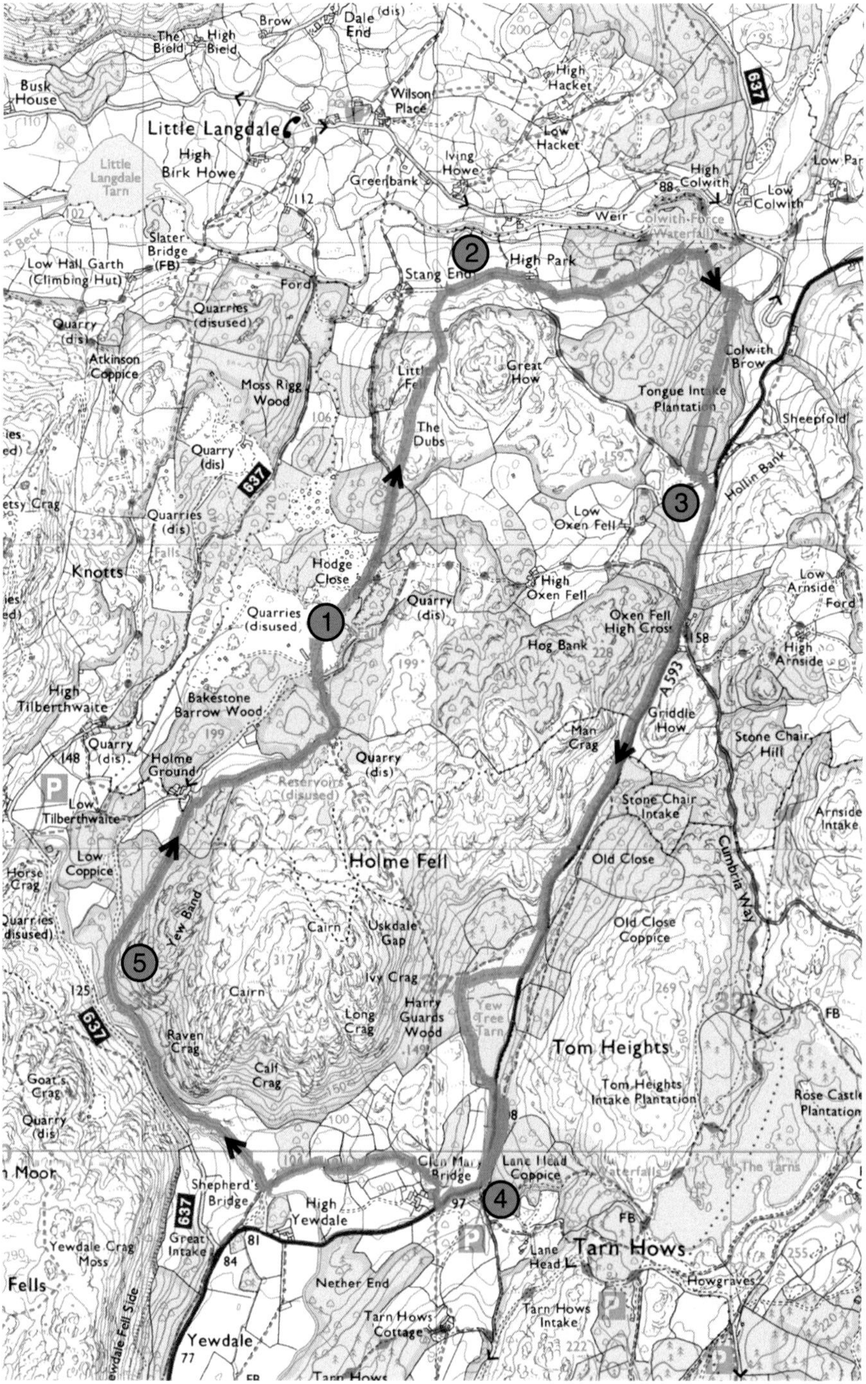
Brow
Dale End
The Bield
High Bield
Busk House
High Hacket
Wilson Place
Little Langdale
Low Hacket
High Birk Howe
Little Langdale Tarn
Iving Howe
Greenbank
High Colwith
Low Colwith
Low Park
Weir
Colwith Force (Waterfall)
Slater Bridge (FB)
Low Hall Garth (Climbing Hut)
Ford
2
High Park
Stang End
Quarries (disused)
Quarry (dis)
Atkinson Coppice
Little Fell
Great How
Colwith Brow
Moss Rigg Wood
Tongue Intake Plantation
The Dubs
Sheepfold
Quarry (dis)
637
Hollin Bank
3
Betsy Crag
Quarries (dis)
Low Oxen Fell
Knotts
Hodge Close
High Oxen Fell
Low Arnside
Quarry (dis)
Ford
Quarries (disused)
1
Oxen Fell High Cross
Hog Bank
High Arnside
A 593
High Tilberthwaite
Bakestone Barrow Wood
Griddle How
Man Crag
Stone Chair Hill
Quarry (dis)
Holme Ground
Quarry (dis)
Reservoirs (disused)
Low Tilberthwaite
Stone Chair Intake
Arnside Intake
Low Coppice
Horse Crag
Holme Fell
Old Close
Cumbria Way
Quarries (disused)
Cairn
Uskdale Gap
Old Close Coppice
Yew Band
5
Ivy Crag
Cairn
Long Crag
Harry Guards Wood
Yew Tree Tarn
Tom Heights
Raven Crag
Calf Crag
Tom Heights Intake Plantation
Goat's Crag
Rose Castle Plantation
Quarry (dis)
Glen Mary Bridge
Lane Head Coppice
The Tarns
Shepherd's Bridge
High Yewdale
4
Tarn Hows
Great Intake
Yewdale Crag Moss
Nether End
Lane Head
Howgraves
Fells
Tarn Hows Cottage
Tarn Hows Intake
Yewdale
Yewdale Fell Side

1 Set out from car park, running north on the designated byway past Hodge Close. After passing through a wooded area you will reach a field gate. The byway heads to the left here but instead follow the waymarked path ahead, which takes you over The Dubs, an area of marshy ground, eventually reaching a stile which leads you downhill to the road from Stang End.

2 Head right and run along the road to the farm (now holiday accommodation) at High Park. Bear left off the road and follow the signs through the farmyard, and across a field to reach a field gate into the woods at Tongue Intake Planation. Stay on the higher path which forms part of the Cumbria Way. After 400 metres of steady descent take a sharp right off the path and follow the signposted bridleway downhill to a footbridge. Once over the bridge follow the signage taking you almost immediately to the right up a steep incline, until you rejoin the lane which you left at High Park.

3 Go left for a short distance towards the A593 and then sharp right onto the signposted public right of way. Follow this path, adjacent to the main road, downhill for 1,200 metres until it bears right, skirting Yew Tree Tarn, and left at the southern end of the tarn, where the path meets the main road. Carefully cross the road and follow the path on the other side until you come to the car park at Glen Mary Bridge.

4 Run on the main A593 road for 200 metres or so until you reach the junction for Yew Tree Farm. Turn right towards the farm and go immediately right again through the field gate signposted for Shepherd's Bridge. Follow this track for 400 metres, through to the bridge on the paved lane up to Hodge Close.

5 Turn right and head north and uphill on the narrow lane for 800 metres, to reach a gate and adjacent footpath on the right-hand side of the road. This path carries on uphill through several gates until you reach the high point of the path and, shortly thereafter and on the descent, the gate to the left into Hodge Close, and back to the car park.

THE BASE OF HODGE CLOSE QUARRY
(© Jumpy James)
www.jumpyjames.co.uk

Trail W5: Broughton Moor

This isolated trail sets out from the high road over Broughton Moor, to the south west of Coniston and Torver, negotiating narrow forest tracks and open fell and moorland on both sides of the River Lickle. It is overlooked on the western side by The Caw (529 metres), a fell which is normally ascended from Seathwaite in the Duddon Valley to the west. The Caw is not to be confused with the significantly higher Caw Fell which is to the north west, in Copeland Borough Council.

Approximate Distance:	7.0 km/4.5 miles.
Terrain:	Narrow footpaths, forestry tracks and a short section of paved country lane.
Severity:	Some steep ascents and descents in addition to the long, steady incline to Natty Bridge.
Approximate Time:	35-50 minutes.
Total Ascent:	284m.
Start of the Trail:	Take the A593 road south from Coniston village, passing through Torver. After a further mile turn right onto the steep Hummer Lane which soon skirts woodland on the right-hand side, just beyond Hummer Bridge. There are dramatic distant views of the sea. Just as the woodland ends, look for a parking place next to footpath signage on the right-hand side of the road.
Map Reference:	SD 245 922 (OS Explorer Map OL6: South-Western Lakes – North Sheet)

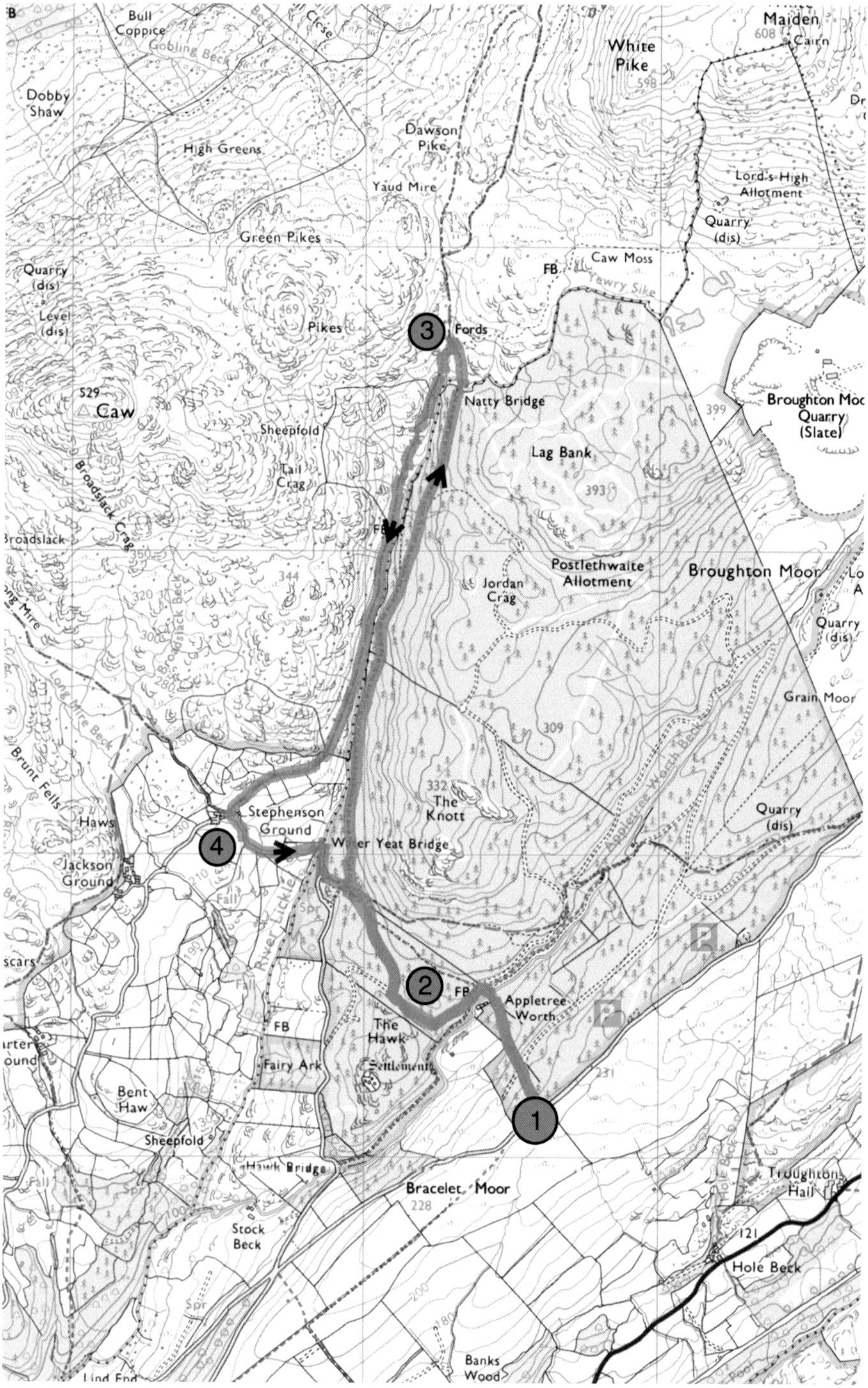
Bull Coppice
Gobling Beck
Dobby Shaw
High Greens
Dawson Pike
Yaud Mire
White Pike
Maiden
Cairn
Lord's High Allotment
Quarry (dis)
Green Pikes
Caw Moss
FB
Yewry Sike
Quarry (dis)
Level (dis)
Pikes
Fords
Natty Bridge
Broughton Moor Quarry (Slate)
529
Caw
Sheepfold
Lag Bank
Tail Crag
Broadslack Crag
Broadslack
Postlethwaite Allotment
Broughton Moor
Jordan Crag
Quarry (dis)
Grain Moor
Long Mire Beck
Brunt Fell
Stephenson Ground
The Knott
Quarry (dis)
Haws
Jackson Ground
Water Yeat Bridge
Appletree Worth Beck
River Lickle
Appletree Worth
The Hawk
Fairy Ark
Settlement
Bent Haw
Sheepfold
Hawk Bridge
Bracelet Moor
Troughton Hall
Stock Beck
Hole Beck
Banks Wood
1
2
3
4

1 From the parking place cross the stile and follow the footpath sign for Appletreeworth. This is a narrow path through woodland, over boardwalks in places, heading across a forestry road and down a steep incline to a stone footbridge. Turn left off the footbridge and then almost immediately right onto a path up a short rise to a forestry track through pine trees. Turn left and follow the track, ignoring the first junction to the left after a short distance. The track curves round to a northerly direction.

2 At the next junction of forestry tracks take a right and continue on as the track emerges from the forest and soon blends with a footpath and heads uphill on a long incline on open heath land for about two kilometres. At the top, negotiate a timber stile and cross the well-maintained timber Natty Bridge across the River Lickle. Continue on uphill for about 100 metres, then take a left at the next junction of paths. Cross a stream and bear left again to follow the terraced path southwards, on the other side of the Lickle.

3 This winding and stony path is undergoing reinforcement by rangers. After one and a half kilometres of downhill running, which requires patience and extra care, the path levels out as it passes through a gate onto farming land, following a wall on the left and then descending to Stephenson Ground Farm.

4 Pass through a field gate at the farm and onto a paved country lane. Turn left and run down the winding lane, crossing Water Yeat Bridge at the bottom of the incline. After a further 50 metres, look for the footpath sign on the left and follow it through a pedestrian gate and into woodland. At a junction of paths, follow the yellow waymark signage on the right which leads you back to the main forestry track. Turn right here and loop round the woodland and back to the footbridge at Appletreeworth. Continue to follow the outward route in reverse, up the steep incline on the narrow path and occasional boardwalks, leading back to Hummer Lane and the parking space.

NATTY BRIDGE ACROSS THE RIVER LICKLE

(The Author)

Trail W6: Coniston to Tarn Hows Cottage

This trail sets out from the village of Coniston and passes through National Trust land including Monk Coniston Estate. The estate was owned by the Marshall family who were contemporaries and associates of Ruskin and Carlyle. James Garth Marshall was the creator of the artificial Tarn Hows which is located a short distance to the north east of the trail. The early part of the route is on the Cumbria Way which covers 70 miles between Ulverston and Carlisle.

The start of this trail is accessible by the 505 Stagecoach bus which travels between Ambleside and Coniston.

Approximate Distance:	6.0 km/3.75 miles.
Terrain:	Clearly defined paths, grass and short sections of road.
Severity:	Elements of testing uphill at the beginning of the run, and up to Tarn Hows Cottage. A steep, windy downhill in the second half, with the exception of the climb up to and through Guards Wood towards the end of the trail.
Approximate Time:	30-50 minutes.
Total Ascent:	264m.
Start of the Trail:	Take the A593 road west from Ambleside, passing through Clappersgate. Turn left at Skelwith Bridge, heading towards Coniston, which is approximately 5 miles to the south. Drive to the centre of the village and turn left onto the B5285 road, signposted for Hawkeshead. Carry on for about 200 metres until you reach Ruskin Avenue on the right-hand side of the road. Park in the main pay car park just beyond this junction.
Map Reference:	NY 303 977 (OS Explorer Map OL7: South-Eastern Lakes – North Sheet)

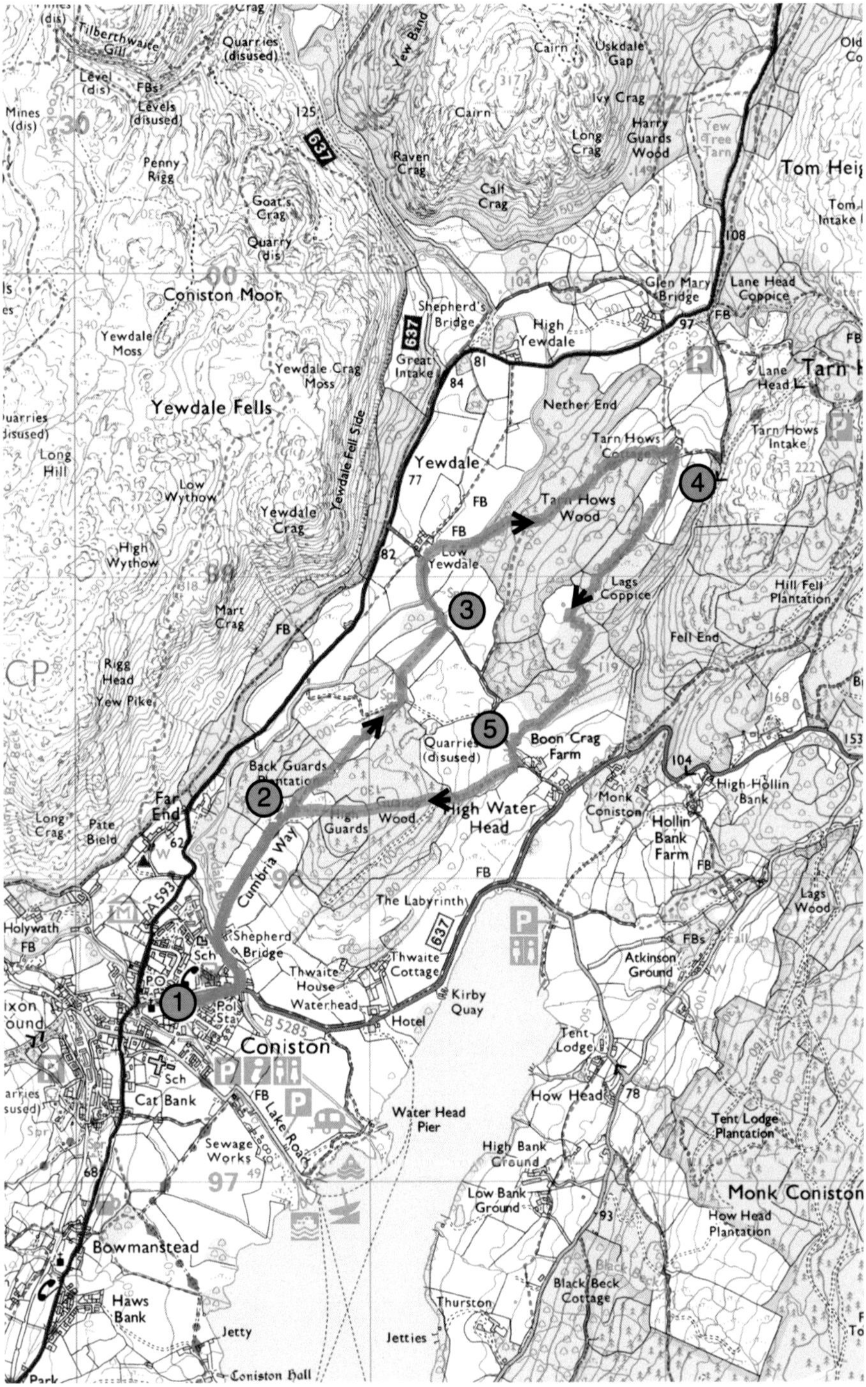
Tilberthwaite Gill
Quarries (disused)
Level (dis)
FBs
Levels (disused)
Mines (dis)
Penny Rigg
Goat's Crag
Quarry (dis)
Yew Band
Cairn
Uskdale Gap
Ivy Crag
Harry Guards Wood
Long Crag
Raven Crag
Calf Crag
Tom Heig
Tom Intake
Coniston Moor
Yewdale Moss
Yewdale Crag Moss
Shepherd's Bridge
Great Intake
High Yewdale
Glen Mary Bridge
Lane Head Coppice
Lane Head
Tarn Hows Intake
Nether End
Tarn Hows Cottage
Yewdale Fells
Long Hill
Low Wythow
High Wythow
Yewdale Crag
Yewdale Fell Side
Yewdale
Tarn Hows Wood
Low Yewdale
Lags Coppice
Hill Fell Plantation
Mart Crag
Fell End
Rigg Head
Yew Pike
Quarries (disused)
Boon Crag Farm
Back Guards Plantation
High Water Head
Guards Wood
High Guards
Far End
Long Crag
Pate Bield
Cumbria Way
Monk Coniston
Hollin Bank Farm
High Hollin Bank
Lags Wood
The Labyrinth
Holywath
Shepherd Bridge
Sch
PO
Thwaite House
Thwaite Cottage
Waterhead
Pol Sta
Kirby Quay
Hotel
Atkinson Ground
Coniston
Tent Lodge
How Head
Cat Bank
Lake Road
Sewage Works
Water Head Pier
High Bank Ground
Tent Lodge Plantation
Low Bank Ground
Monk Coniston
How Head Plantation
Bowmanstead
Black Beck Cottage
Haws Bank
Thurston
Jetty
Jetties
Coniston Hall
1
2
3
4
5

1 Run down the Hawkshead road from the car park until you reach the road bridge over Yewdale Beck after about 150 metres. Turn left just before the bridge and continue along the road signposted for Ambleside, passing the Sports Centre, until you reach Shepherds Bridge on the right, after 200 metres. Cross the bridge on the path and almost immediately follow the signage taking you on a sharp left through a gate and into fields. Follow the clearly defined path which passes the Grade 2 listed 19th Century Gothic folly of the Marshall family's fox hound 'kennel'. Continue through the adjacent gate and head uphill.

2 Shortly you will pass the junction with the return path on your right. Carry on uphill on the main path, passing through several gates. You will come to another junction leading to the woods on the right but continue on the main path, taking a slight downhill over meadow, through a six-bar field gate and across a further field onto the farm track between Low Yewdale and Boon Crag Farm.

3 Turn left here and continue on the enclosed track towards Low Yewdale. After 250 metres or so the track crosses the beck over a bridge to the left, but instead follow the signage ahead and carry straight on through the gate into a field. Skirt the field on the left-hand side arcing to the right until you reach a kissing gate in the far corner which leads to a clear, stony path through Tarn Hows wood. Continue on the path and up a very steep section leading you to Tarn Hows Cottage.

4 Pass through the gate at the top, next to the cottage, and turn immediately right through another gate, following the signage onto a meadow. After negotiating a further gate, pass along the edge of Lags Coppice, through a wall gap and down the winding, occasionally rocky, path. You will see Lake Coniston in the distance as you negotiate the steep hill to the farm track leading to Boon Crag Farm.

5 Turn left at the track and look for the stile on the right just before the farm buildings. Cross the stile and run uphill towards Guards Wood. The waymarked path becomes steeper as you pass through the impressive, cathedral-like plantation of fir trees. Beyond the ridge there is a very steep downhill section over tree roots to a gate in the wall. Once through the gate, and clear of the woods, carry on for a further 100 metres or so until you reach the junction with the main path up from Coniston. Head left and retrace your steps past the folly, onto the road and back to the car park.

THE DESCENT PAST THE MARSHALL FAMILY FOX HOUND 'KENNEL'
(© Jumpy James)
www.jumpyjames.co.uk

THE CENTRAL AREA

Trail C1: Burneside and Cowan Head

Burneside is a small village between Staveley and Kendal, which is the home of the long-established James Cropper Paper Mill. The mill manufactures unique, custom-made paper products for a number of the world's leading luxury brands, and for many art galleries and designers.

The trail follows a short section of the Dales Way (80 Miles between Ilkley in West Yorkshire and Bowness-on-Windermere), before heading off through fields and along country lanes, with alternative options for the route back from Bowston.

The start of this trail is accessible by both the 555 Stagecoach bus from Kendal, and the Lakes Line.

Approximate Distance:	7.0 km/4.5 miles.
Terrain:	Fields, footpaths and road.
Severity:	Fairly level throughout.
Approximate Time:	35-50 minutes.
Total Ascent:	111m.
Start of the Trail:	Start from the centre of Burneside. If you are using a car, park on Main Street, near the Jolly Anglers Inn, just beyond the railway station.
Map Reference:	NY 505 957 (OS Explorer Map OL7: South-Eastern Lakes - North Sheet)

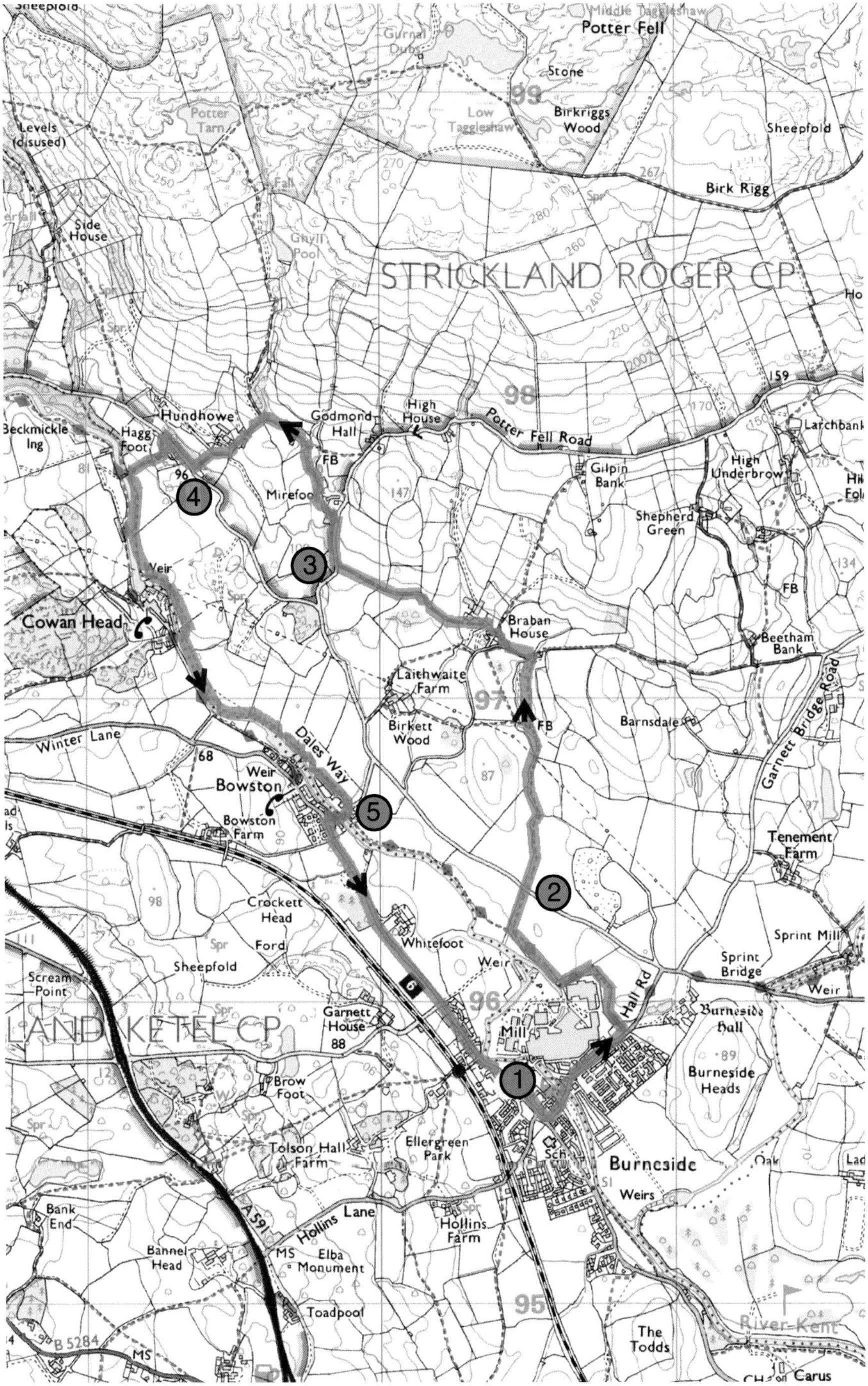
Potter Fell
Stone
Birkriggs Wood
Low Taggleshaw
Gurnal Dubs
Potter Tarn
Levels (disused)
Sheepfold
Birk Rigg
Side House
Ghyll Pool
STRICKLAND ROGER CP
Hundhowe
Hagg Foot
Beckmickle Ing
Godmond Hall
High House
Potter Fell Road
FB
Mirefoot
Gilpin Bank
High Underbrow
Larchbank
Shepherd Green
Weir
Cowan Head
Braban House
Beetham Bank
Laithwaite Farm
Birkett Wood
Barnsdale
Garnett Bridge Road
Winter Lane
Dales Way
Bowston
Bowston Farm
Tenement Farm
Crockett Head
Whitefoot
Sprint Mill
Sprint Bridge
Ford
Sheepfold
Scream Point
Hall Rd
Mill
Burneside Hall
Burneside Heads
Garnett House
LAND KETEL CP
Brow Foot
Tolson Hall Farm
Ellergreen Park
Sch
Burneside
Weirs
Bank End
Hollins Lane
Hollins Farm
A591
Bannel Head
MS
Elba Monument
Toadpool
B 5284
The Todds
River Kent
Carus
1
2
3
4
5

1 Jog down the road in the direction of Kendal and turn left at Hall Road, passing the village store and heading across the recently constructed Ford Bridge over the River Kent. After approximately 200 metres take the footpath between a wall and fence, running parallel to the left-hand side of the road. Very shortly you will see the footpath sign directing you on a hard left and onto the Dales Way which skirts the fenced-in industrial estate of the Cropper works.

You will eventually come to a gate which takes you onto a field next to the river. Follow the clear path along the field (the lower section is easier, especially in damp weather) to reach a timber gate in the left-hand corner. Do not go through the gate but instead turn sharp right and follow the less defined public footpath in a northerly direction with the wall on your left, to reach a stile onto a country lane in the left-hand field corner.

2 Immediately cross the lane to another stile, and onto pasture. Here the right of way is less distinct but stay close to the wall on the left as you pass through three fields, curving round to the left at the end of the third one to reach a large metal field gate. Turn left here, onto an unpaved country lane, and continue for a short distance until you see the yellow way marker directing you to the right, just before a cottage. Follow the bridleway as it sweeps left, to the rear of Braban House. The footpath crosses the rear garden of the house to a gate in the right-hand far corner. The signage will take you diagonally left over another field to a gate and onto an enclosed bridleway. Follow this for 600 metres until it reaches the Potter Fell Road.

3 Turn right and run up the road for 150 metres, passing a layby, and then take a left off the road and onto the footpath signposted for Mirefoot. Follow this constructed farm track as it wends its way up the increasingly steep hill past holiday cottages on the left. Shortly you will see a waymarked yellow sign directing walkers to the right and up to Potter Tarn.

Ignore this and turn immediately left through a gate and onto a narrow, enclosed path, descending to another gate and into the farmyard at Low Hundhowe. Go straight ahead downhill, past some traditional farm buildings, through a metal gate and onto the concrete farm access track. The track passes the entrance to High Hundhowe, and continues down to the back road to Burneside.

4 Turn right along the road and in 100 metres, just beyond Hag Foot, take a left and follow the signage guiding you behind the buildings and onto an enclosed path to the right, and downhill to the River Kent. Just before the river, follow the Dales Way signage onto meadow and run along past the small private golf course at Cowan Head. Continue on the pleasant grassy meadow at the edge of the river, past the Cowan Head flatted development with its dramatic river views, and on through fields, across stiles and through gates. Just before Bowston the path passes through a gate and along the edge of woodland to reach the road into the village. Turn right onto the road.

5 At this point you have the choice of crossing over the road bridge at Bowston and heading up to the main road, turning left and following the footpath on the other side for one kilometre, until you reach Burneside, and the starting point.

The alternative is to turn left just before the road bridge and continue on the Dales Way across more fields at the edge of the river, until the route reconnects with your outward journey, taking you through the timber gate in the field corner, to the path round the industrial estate, and back along the road to the start of the run.

The advantage of the road option is that you complete a full loop, although some runners may prefer the path over the fields on the Dales Way.

SKIRTING THE CROPPER INDUSTRIAL ESTATE ON THE WAY FROM BURNESIDE (Lois Blamire)

Trail C2: The River Kent Loop

This trail (together with Trails C7 and C10) sets out from Staveley Mill Yard which is a four-acre site comprised of over 20 retail and industrial units, in the centre of Staveley village. By-passed by the A591, Staveley is situated equidistant between Kendal and Windermere and is within easy reach of the Central Lake District. The yard was originally the industrial centre of the village, utilising the River Kent, which passes to the east, to provide power for wood turning, principally the supply of bobbins for the cotton manufacturing industry in Lancashire.

The trail combines path and road and passes through Beckmickle Ing, an area of woodland owned by the Woodland Trust, which contains a rich mix of deciduous trees and a diverse range of ground flora. It has been designated an area of Great Landscape Value. The trail emerges from the woodland and returns along the banks of the River Kent and back to Staveley on the Dales Way, which covers 80 Miles between Ilkley in West Yorkshire and Bowness-on-Windermere.

The start of this trail is accessible by both the 555 Stagecoach which travels between Kendal and Keswick, and the Lakes Line.

Approximate Distance:	6.5 km/4.0 miles.
Terrain:	Road and paths throughout, with a mixture of rocky and grassy sections
Severity:	Steady climb on the road near the start of the run and then, once downhill, fairly level thereafter.
Approximate Time:	30-45 minutes.
Total Ascent:	112m.
Start of the Trail:	Park in the Mill Yard in the centre of Staveley village.
Map Reference:	NY 470 984 (OS Explorer Map OL7: South-Eastern Lakes – North Sheet)

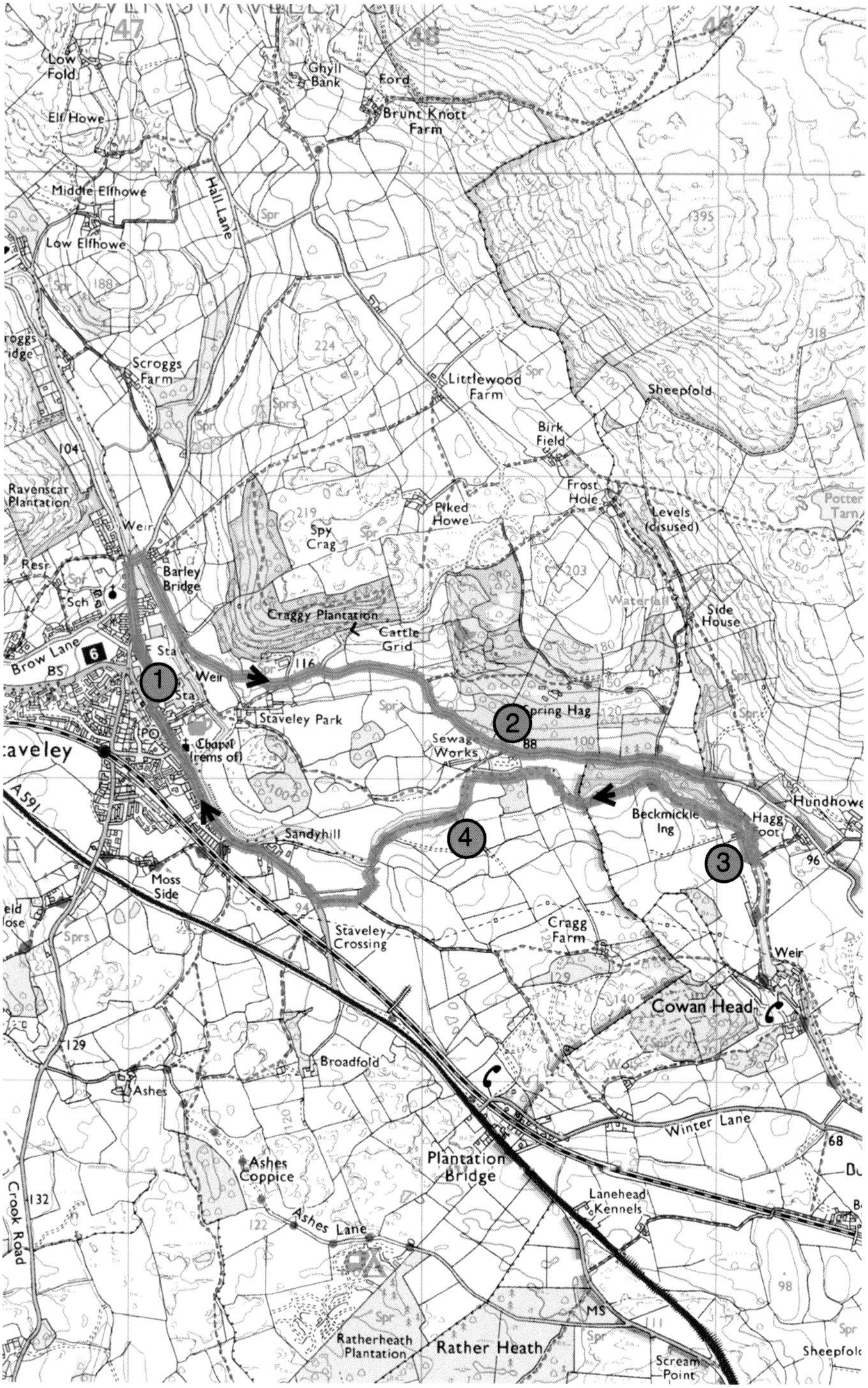
Low Fold
Ghyll Bank
Ford
Elf Howe
Brunt Knott Farm
Middle Elfhowe
Hall Lane
Low Elfhowe
Scroggs Farm
Littlewood Farm
Sheepfold
Birk Field
Ravenscar Plantation
Frost Hole
Levels (disused)
Potter Tarn
Weir
Spy Crag
Piked Howe
Barley Bridge
Craggy Plantation
Cattle Grid
Waterfall
Side House
Brow Lane
Sch
Sta
Staveley Park
Spring Hag
Sewage Works
Chapel (rems of)
Staveley
A591
Hundhowe
Beckmickle Ing
Hagg Foot
Sandyhill
Moss Side
Staveley Crossing
Cragg Farm
Cowan Head
Broadfold
Ashes
Winter Lane
Plantation Bridge
Ashes Coppice
Crook Road
Lanehead Kennels
Ashes Lane
Ratherheath Plantation
Rather Heath
Scream Point
Sheepfold
1
2
3
4

1 Turn right as you leave the Mill Yard, and head along Back Lane, merging with the Kentmere Road after about 200 metres. In a further 250 metres, turn right over Barley Bridge and then right again onto the back road towards Burneside and the A6. Continue on the road as it heads uphill, ignoring the lane to the right into a farm and the Craggy road to the left at the top of the hill. Carry on downhill until you reach the sewage works. At this point you will meet the alternative route from Staveley, through Staveley Park[8].

2 Continue on the road and shortly you will come across Beckmickle Ing, the wooded area on the right-hand side. Ignore the entrance at the beginning of the Ing and continue along past two sections of timber fencing across gaps in the stone wall. At the third section, there is signposted access into the woodland. Follow this and proceed downhill, taking care not to trip on tree roots.

As the path nears the River Kent it turns left across a small timber bridge. Carry on as the path runs adjacent to a wall on the left. Within a short distance you will come to the end of the woods. Go through the gate and turn right over the reconstructed bridge across the river, which replaced the makeshift bridge destroyed by the floods in 2015.

3 Turn right on the other side of the Kent and head towards a partially restored barn, passing through two adjacent field gates. The path becomes rocky and winding as it passes alongside the river, where great care is needed when the river is in spate, and heads uphill to reach a field gate. Go through the gate and follow the clear path over wall stiles and across fields until you reach another area of enclosed woodland.

Negotiate a wall stile in the right-hand corner, adjacent to the river, and run the short distance through the woods adjacent to the wall on the right to reach another wall stile. The path then continues through a field next to the river, looping left, round to a wall gap, and then right to a field gate into a meadow.

4 Follow the path on the right-hand side of the meadow to reach a farm track between walls, and continue on to a kissing gate. Go left through another kissing gate (ignoring the original right of way through Sandyhill Farm) and follow the path through a wall gap and over the next field to reach another kissing gate. Turn right here onto the enclosed path, and carry on the short distance to a field gate which leads you onto the road into the south end of Staveley. Run into the village on the pavement, crossing the new road bridge adjacent to the Eagle and Child Inn, and heading along the main street, back to the Mill Yard.

PARTIALLY RESTORED BARN ON THE RIVER KENT FOOTPATH
(Roger Blamire)

[8] The alternative route is described in reverse in Trail C7: Potter Tarn

Trail C3: Gamblesmire Lane and Cunswick Scar

This trail takes in winding lanes and the limestone Cunswick Scar which is listed in the Scout Scar chapter of Wainwright's 'The Outlying Fells of Lakeland'. The scar offers extensive views of the Central Lakeland fells from the large limestone cairn at the top of Cunswick Fell.

Approximate Distance:	10.0 km/6.0 miles.
Terrain:	Road, paths and farm access tracks.
Severity:	Generally easy, with a short ascent onto Cunswick Scar
Approximate Time:	55-75 minutes.
Total Ascent:	249m.
Start of the Trail:	The trail starts at the south end of Ratherheath Lane, which is accessible off the south west side of the A591, between Staveley and Kendal. Enter the lane opposite the junction to Burneside, and park in the layby at the far end, next to the B5284 Bowness to Kendal road.
Map Reference:	NY 478 953 (OS Explorer Map OL7: South-Eastern Lakes – North Sheet)

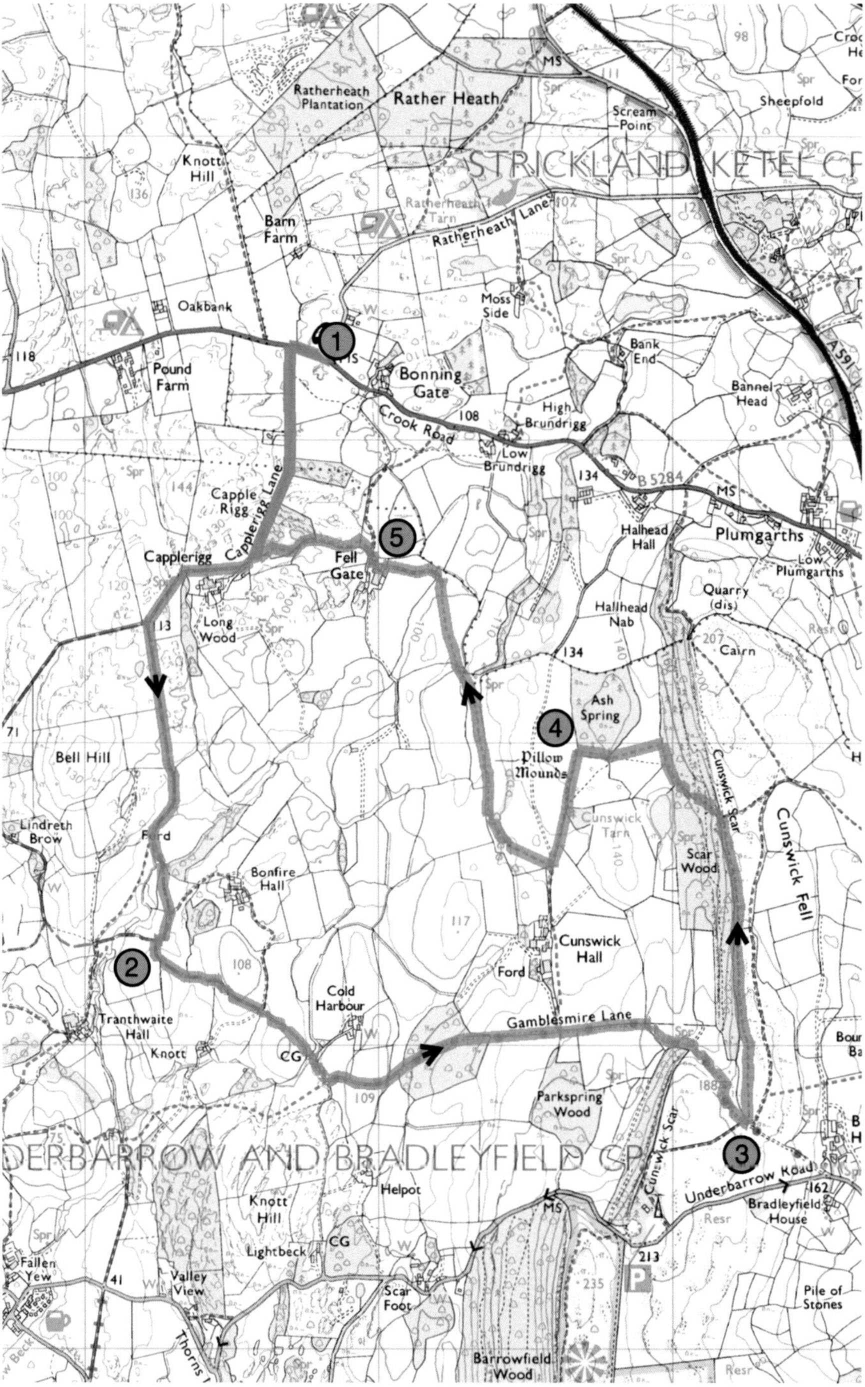

Ratherheath Plantation
Rather Heath
Scream Point
Sheepfold
STRICKLAND KETEL CP
Knott Hill
Ratherheath Tarn
Ratherheath Lane
Barn Farm
Moss Side
Oakbank
Pound Farm
1
Bonning Gate
Bank End
Bannel Head
A591
Crook Road
High Brundrigg
Low Brundrigg
B 5284
Capple Rigg
Capplerigg Lane
Capplerigg
5
Fell Gate
Halhead Hall
Plumgarths
Low Plumgarths
Quarry (dis)
Long Wood
Hallhead Nab
Cairn
Ash Spring
4
Pillow Mounds
Bell Hill
Cunswick Scar
Cunswick Fell
Lindreth Brow
Ford
Cunswick Tarn
Scar Wood
Bonfire Hall
Cunswick Hall
2
Ford
Tranthwaite Hall
Cold Harbour
Knott
Gamblesmire Lane
Parkspring Wood
3
DERBARROW AND BRADLEYFIELD CP
Underbarrow Road
Helpot
Bradleyfield House
Knott Hill
Lightbeck
Fallen Yew
Valley View
Scar Foot
Pile of Stones
Thorns
Barrowfield Wood

1 Set out from the layby, running south to the B5284. Turn right at the junction, taking care from traffic and, after 100m, look for the junction with Capplerigg Lane, on the other side of the road. Run down the lane which veers right after 800 metres. At the junction with the track leading into Capplerigg Farm look for the signpost to Lindreth Brow on the right. Follow this track through a gate, bearing left after 200 metres, until you come to another junction of paths.

Ignore the signpost to Lindreth Brow at this point and take the left-hand reconstructed track of slate chips which travels in a straight line for 600 metres, eventually veering slightly to the right and across a ford. If the stream is in spate, cross at a small stone footbridge on the left-hand side of the path. Continue to a field gate and traverse the next field on a farm track until you come to another signpost.

2 Take the path signposted to Underbarrow which takes a sharp right and almost immediately a sharp left onto a track between hedgerows. Follow this track up and over an incline, and down to a paved lane. The lane leads to a gate and a track over another field, and turns sharp left into Gamblemire Lane.

Follow the lane as it undulates through woods and along fields, passing the entrance to Cunswick Hall Farm. The lane continues through a field gate and bends to the right, passing close to a redundant stone lime kiln, and ascends the short incline to Cunswick Scar. Pass through the wall gap and turn left onto moorland on the ridge of the scar.

3 Follow the path along the moorland, staying close to Scar Wood on the left. After one kilometre you will come to a wooden kissing gate which leads you onto a downhill path and diagonally through the wood, following the edge of the trees at the foot of the hill. As you descend, you will see Cunswick Tarn behind you to the left. Pass through the gate at the bottom of Scar Wood and follow the waymark signage, taking a left across the field to the edge of Ash Spring copse. Pass through the copse on the footpath, crossing stone stiles at the entrance and exit.

4 Turn sharp left on leaving the copse and follow the path towards Cunswick Hall Farm. Just before the wall gap into the farm look for the footpath sign which takes you right, across fields and along the edge of a hedgerow, leading to a gate into an adjacent field on the left. Continue following the hedge row on the other side of the gate and look for the gap at the far left corner of the field. Once through this continue following the waymark signage across another field and down to the track which heads left into Fell Gate Farm.

5 Pass through the field gate into the farmyard. The signage will lead you through the farm to reach a junction of paths. Take the left-hand path and follow the track which leads you past a copse on the right, up to a field gate, and back onto Capplerigg Lane. Turn right at the lane and retrace your steps to the main road and Ratherheath Lane.

THE LIME KILN ON THE PATH UP TO CUNSWICK SCAR
(© Jumpy James)
www.jumpyjames.co.uk

Trail C4: School Knott from Ings

This trail goes across typical South Lakes terrain. School Knott (230 metres) is a grassy mound less well known than Orrest Head but with equally splendid views of Lake Windermere and the Central Fells. There is a section of the trail taking in the Dales Way (80 Miles between Ilkley in West Yorkshire and Bowness-on-Windermere).

The start of this trail is accessible by the 555 Stagecoach bus which travels between Kendal and Keswick.

Approximate Distance:	9.0 km/5.5 miles.
Terrain:	Mainly grassy paths across pasture, with some road surfaces. There are sections of poorly defined path but generally there is good signage according with the map. Be prepared for some grazing land used for sheep and cattle for most of year.
Severity:	Some undulating terrain with a steep incline and descent on grass to and from the summit of School Knott, and a pleasant downhill to Hag End Farm on the second half of the run.
Approximate Time:	45-60 minutes.
Total Ascent:	231m.
Start of the Trail:	Ings is located on the A591 approximately half-way between Staveley and Windermere. Take the narrow road into the centre of Ings from the west and park on-street, next to the Waterside Inn.
Map Reference:	NY 445 987 (OS Explorer Map OL7: South-Eastern Lakes – North Sheet)

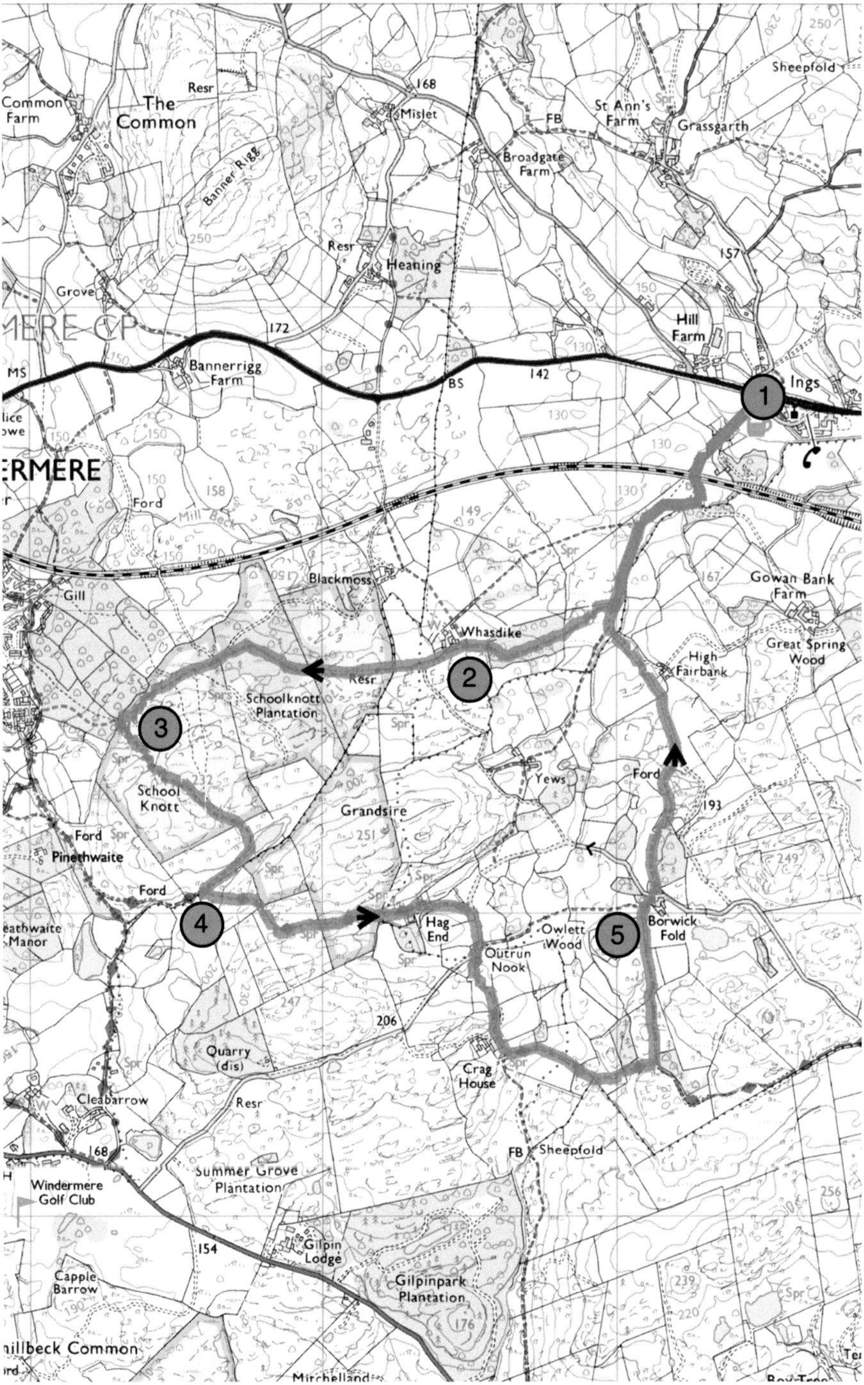

Common Farm
The Common
Resr
Banner Rigg
168
Mislet
Broadgate Farm
FB
St Ann's Farm
Grassgarth
Sheepfold
Heaning
Grove
172
157
Hill Farm
Bannerrigg Farm
MS
BS
142
Ings
1
ERMERE
Ford
Mill Beck
158
149
Blackmoss
Gill
Gowan Bank Farm
Whasdike
Great Spring Wood
High Fairbank
2
Resr
3
Schoolknott Plantation
School Knott
232
Grandsire
251
Yews
Ford
193
249
Ford
Pinethwaite
Ford
4
Hag End
Owlett Wood
5
Borwick Fold
Outrun Nook
206
247
230
Quarry (dis)
Crag House
Cleabarrow
Resr
168
FB
Sheepfold
Windermere Golf Club
Summer Grove Plantation
256
154
Gilpin Lodge
Capple Barrow
Gilpinpark Plantation
239
220
176
Mitchelland

1 From the inn, take the paved lane off to the left passing some houses on both sides, and heading through a field gate and under the Lakes Railway Line. The lane veers right and then left after the railway bridge and in 400 metres you will see the footpath sign on the right which directs you across grazing land and through a pedestrian gate into woodland. Follow the clear path through the woods to a further gate at the other side. The path becomes rocky for a section before it reaches the paved lane at Whasdyke Farm.

2 Turn left onto the lane and continue on, ignoring a junction to the left. Cross a cattle grid just before the road takes a sharp bend to the right. At this point carry straight on, off the lane, and follow the path across pasture, past a red roofed barn and into another section of woodland with a pedestrian gate on entry. The path becomes very wet and rocky in places but is well defined and you will soon reach another gate on exit taking you onto the open meadow below School Knott. Continue on for 400 metres until you see a high timber pedestrian gate in the wall to the right, which provides access for the main path up School Knott from Windermere.

3 Carry on for a short distance then turn left and follow the grassy path uphill. The path becomes less defined as it heads to the summit of School Knott. Enjoy the views at the summit before you carry straight on and down to a gate in a wall. Pass through the opening and bend right alongside a small tarn. As you head away from the tarn, look for the gate in the wall on the left where you will join the Dales Way.

4 Pass through the gate and follow the less clearly defined path uphill and slightly to the left between hillocks. The path becomes very clear again as it heads through gates and follows waymarker signage down the easy descent to Hag End Farm. The right of way passes between the former farm buildings and the signage directs you to a road junction beyond the farm. Take a right here, continuing on the Dales Way for the short distance to Outrun Nook.

Bear right to reach a gate and signage opposite the buildings and skirt the next field on the left, heading towards Crag House Farm. Turn left through the field gate as you leave the farm, and pass along the left-hand edge of the next field, to a further gate. Continue on the Dales Way past gorse bushes until you reach a three-way sign. Take the left-hand fork and follow the less defined path to Borwick Fold.

5 At Borwick Fold, turn left at the buildings and right at a paved lane. Very shortly turn immediately left again before a barn, following the footpath signage across stiles and alongside the woodland on the right. Enter the wood through a stile and high gate and follow the path to reach another stile and high gate on exit. Continue downhill next to the wood on the left and bear slightly right in the direction of the solar-panelled roofs of the former farm buildings at High Fairbank. Go onto the lane and continue downhill and back to Ings.

LAKE WINDERMERE FROM THE SUMMIT OF SCHOOL KNOTT
(Lois Blamire)

Trail C5: Winster and Lambhowe Plantation

This trail passes over the rolling countryside, through the wooded areas and across the open fields typical of South Lakeland. It is easily accessible by car from Windermere and Bowness. Winster is the home of the popular Brown Horse Inn where the majority of the meats are reared and vegetables grown on the Brown Horse Estate.

Approximate Distance:	6.0 km/3.75 miles.
Terrain:	Paths, tracks and road.
Severity:	Undulating, with some short, steep sections which are not unduly demanding.
Approximate Time:	35-45 minutes.
Total Ascent:	194m.
Start of the Trail:	From Bowness-on-Windermere take the A5074 from the centre of town, heading south, past the Royal Oak Hotel on the left (which marks the end of the 80 mile long Dales Way from Ilkley). Stay on the main road, passing the junctions signposted for the Windermere Ferry and Blackwell House, and continue through the village of Winster. After a further kilometre, park in the layby on the right-hand side of the road, just beyond the junction with a country lane on the left.
Map Reference:	NY 423 926 (OS Explorer Map OL7: South-Eastern Lakes – North Sheet)

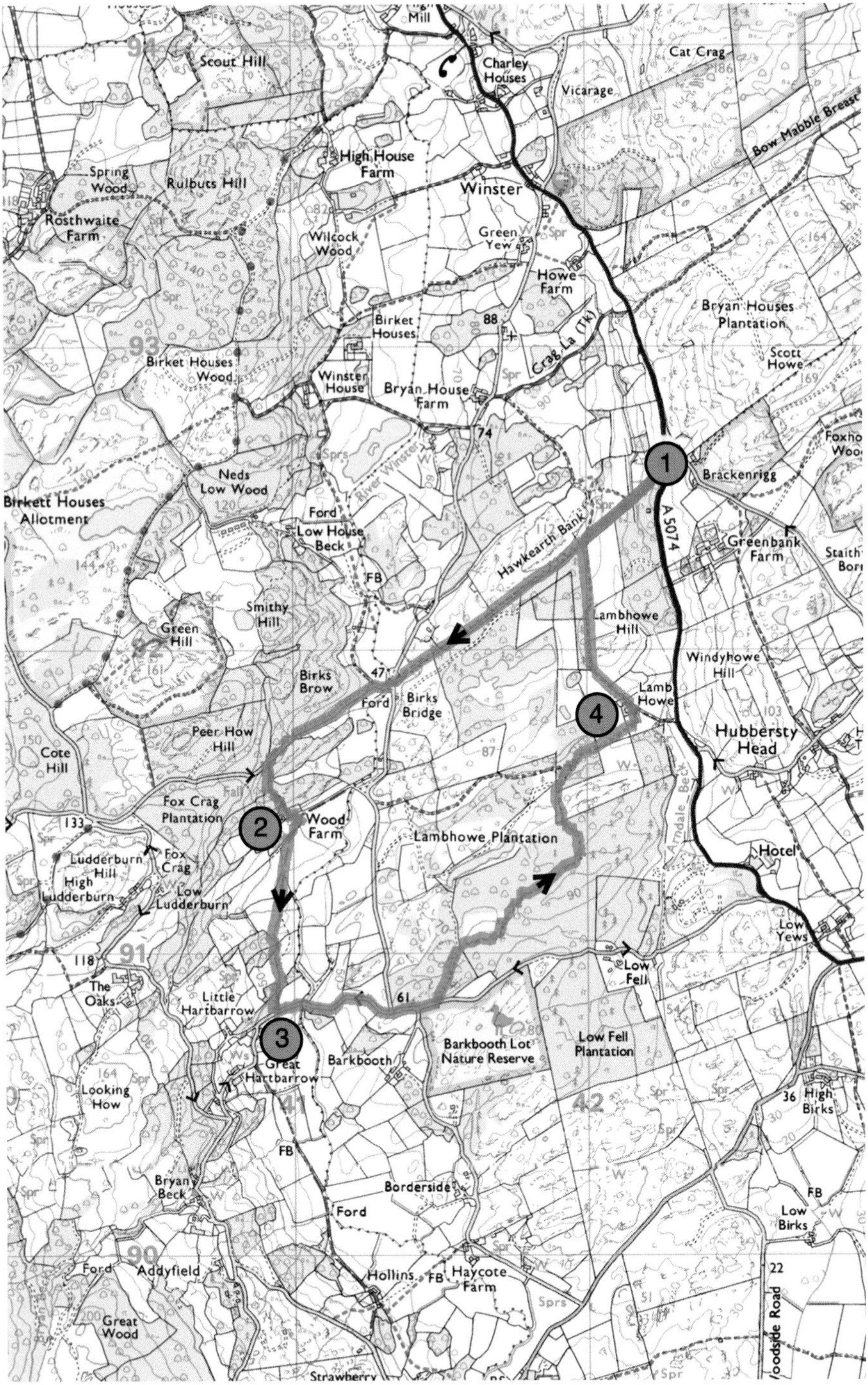
Scout Hill
Charley Houses
Cat Crag
Vicarage
Bow Mabble Breast
High House Farm
Spring Wood
Rulbuts Hill
Winster
Rosthwaite Farm
Wilcock Wood
Green Yew
Howe Farm
Bryan Houses Plantation
Birket Houses
Crag La (Tk)
Scott Howe
Birket Houses Wood
Winster House
Bryan House Farm
Neds Low Wood
River Winster
1
Brackenrigg
Birkett Houses Allotment
Ford
Low House Beck
Hawkearth Bank
A 5074
Greenbank Farm
Smithy Hill
Lambhowe Hill
Green Hill
Windyhowe Hill
Birks Brow
Birks Bridge
Lamb Howe
4
Peer How Hill
Hubbersty Head
Cote Hill
Fox Crag Plantation
2
Wood Farm
Lambhowe Plantation
Hotel
Ludderburn Hill
High Ludderburn
Fox Crag
Low Ludderburn
Low Yews
Low Fell
The Oaks
Little Hartbarrow
3
Great Hartbarrow
Barkbooth
Barkbooth Lot Nature Reserve
Low Fell Plantation
Looking How
High Birks
Bryan Beck
Borderside
Ford
Low Birks
Addyfield
Hollins
Haycote Farm
Great Wood
Woodside Road
Strawberry

1 Follow the footpath sign for Birks Bridge directly from the layby, passing through the field boundary gate and left through another gate to turn right onto the clear but muddy path downhill, and across a short section of boardwalk. Continue straight ahead at the waymarks on the next gate, heading uphill with a wall on your left, and over a ladder stile. The grassy path leads you over the incline, continuing straight ahead on a gentle downhill section to a wall stile, and onto a paved country lane.

Cross the lane and take the stone footbridge at the ford immediately ahead. Follow the paved lane up a long, winding incline of approximately 500 metres. Just after the junction with a forestry path on the right, go off the lane at the signposted 'Albert's Amble' footpath on the left. This is a steep downhill, which is rocky in places, leading to the picturesque Wood Farm.

2 Turn left at the farm and then shortly right, following the waymarks round a barn, and avoiding the more obvious looking access to a field on the left. The enclosed path continues to a gate and into a muddy and occasionally rutted field. Cross a small planked bridge over a stream in the middle of the field and make for the wall gap ahead. The path becomes less defined as you head right and then left over the next field to reach a gate into a copse. The enclosed path continues down to a paved country lane.

3 Turn left and follow the lane uphill. At the first junction of lanes, after 400 metres, carry straight on, following the road sign for Kendal and Bowland Bridge and, at the next junction, continue straight ahead for Kendal and Crosthwaite. Shortly you will come to a footpath sign for 'Lambhowe 1 mile' at a gate on the left, taking you off road and through the densely wooded area of Lambhowe Plantation. After 200 metres, go right to follow the waymark sign at a timber kissing gate.

Continue on the strategically waymarked trail through the plantation until you reach a wall stile leading to an open meadow. Skirt the meadow on the left to reach a ladder stile and continue through more woodland to reach a timber gate into a field. Cross the field, go through the field gate and loop round the farmhouse to reach the access track to Lambhowe farm, with its pretty, enclosed courtyard.

4 Do not enter the farm but cross the track and take the path straight ahead and uphill to a field gate. Follow the waymarks across the field to a ladder stile in the far right-hand corner. Negotiate the stile onto an enclosed path with high forestry fencing on the left-hand side. After 200 metres you will come to a timber pedestrian gate on the right into another field. Remain on the left-hand side of the field to arrive at a stone stile in the far corner. Cross the stile, onto the outgoing footpath for Birks Bridge. Turn right, head down to the valley floor and then up the other side, over the board walk, through the gates and back to the starting point.

WOOD FARM
(The Author)

Trail C6: Cunswick Fell

This is a steep trail from the northern edge of Kendal, crossing the A591 dual carriageway in both directions, and encircling the popular upland pasture next to Cunswick Scar.

The start of this trail is accessible by the 555 Stagecoach bus from Kendal to Keswick.

Approximate Distance: 8.0 km/5.0 miles.

Terrain: Paths, grass and some sections of road.

Severity: Generally steep, levelling out on the grassy meadow round the fell.

Approximate Time: 40-60 minutes.

Total Ascent: 262m.

Start of the Trail: From the Windermere Road to the north of Kendal, head south and uphill on Queens Road for 400 metres, and park at the foot of the path signed for Helsfell Nab on the right-hand side of the road.

Map Reference: SD 511 928 (OS Explorer Map OL7: South-Eastern Lakes – North Sheet)

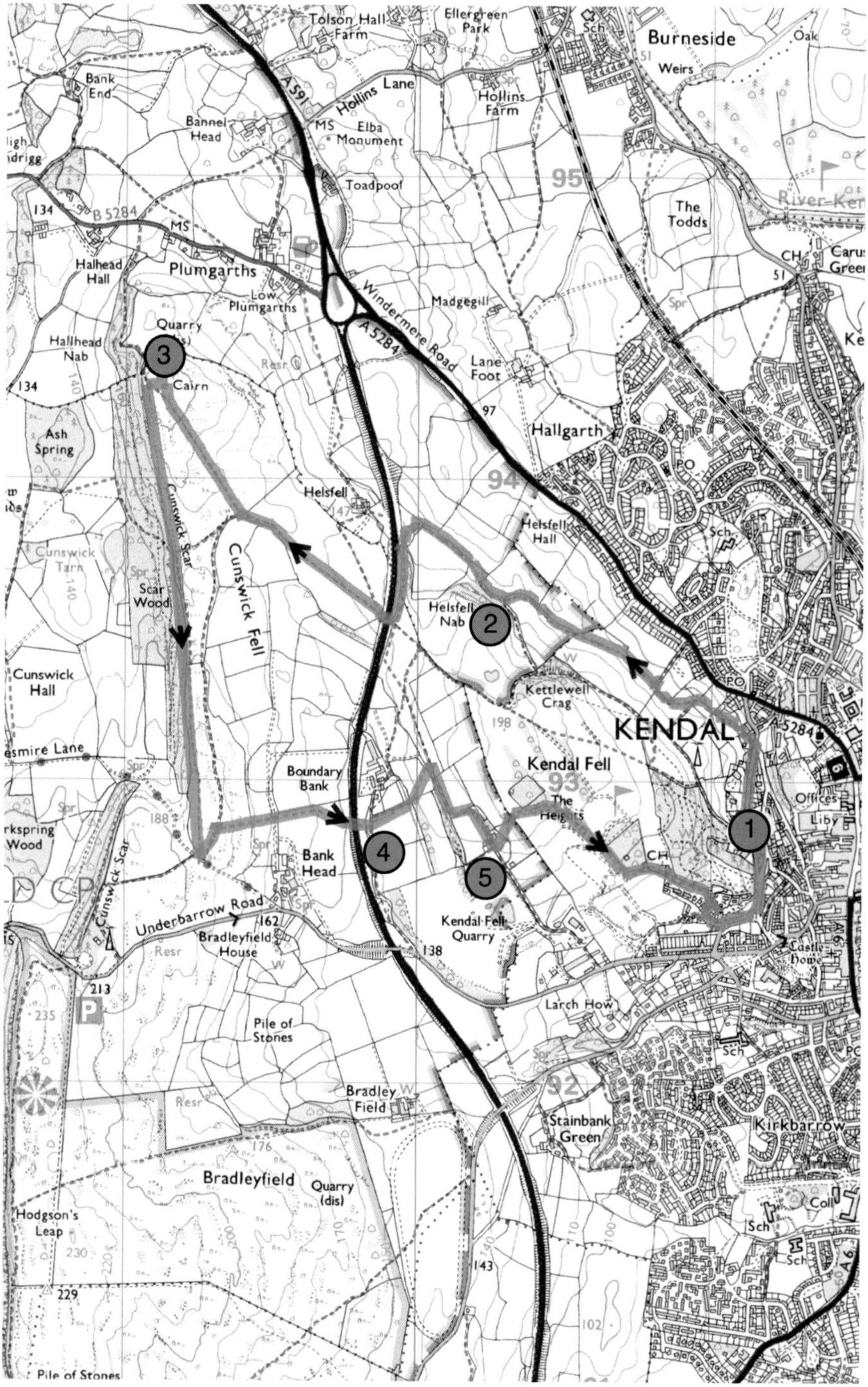

Tolson Hall Farm
Ellergreen Park
Burneside
Weirs
Oak
Bank End
Hollins Lane
Hollins Farm
Bannel Head
MS
Elba Monument
A591
95
Toadpool
The Todds
River Kent
134
B 5284
MS
Halhead Hall
Plumgarths
Low Plumgarths
Windermere Road
A 5284
Madgegill
CH
Carus Green
Quarry (dis)
Hallhead Nab
3
Cairn
Resr
Lane Foot
97
134
Hallgarth
Ash Spring
Helsfell
94
PO
Cunswick Scar
Cunswick Fell
Helsfell Hall
Sch
Cunswick Tarn
Scar Wood
Helsfell Nab
2
Cunswick Hall
Kettlewell Crag
198
KENDAL
A 5284
Boundary Bank
Kendal Fell
93
The Heights
Offices
Liby
188
1
Bank Head
4
5
CH
Underbarrow Road
162
Bradleyfield House
Kendal Fell Quarry
Resr
138
Castle Howe
213
235
Larch How
Pile of Stones
92
Resr
Bradley Field
Stainbank Green
Sch
Kirkbarrow
176
Bradleyfield
Quarry (dis)
Coll
Hodgson's Leap
230
Sch
Sch
143
229
102
Pile of Stones

1 Run back down Queens Road towards the Windermere Road for 300 metres, to reach a footpath sign on the left-hand side of the road. Take this path as it heads uphill between houses, through gates and onto pasture and grazing land. When you reach a wall gap follow the right-hand of two waymark signs and cross the field diagonally to reach a double gate at a group of trees. Once through the gate, run pass the footpath sign at the junction with a path up from the Windermere Road and carry straight on across the pasture to a metal kissing gate. From this gate the clear path directs you to a gate and stile in the left-hand field corner below Helsfell Nab.

2 Turn right onto the path through woodland and cross a wall stile into a field at the far end. From here the path directs you across the field to a wall gap on the left-hand side of two semi-detached stone barns. Once through the gap head left on the path and up the steep hill, curving round to follow a wall and fence, with the A591 dual carriageway below you to the right. Pass through a copse with gates on entry and exit and continue to the pedestrian bridge across the main road.

At the far end of the bridge pass through a gate and turn right to head through a second gate leading to a large, open field. Follow the left-hand of two waymarks and take the well-defined path diagonally across the meadow until you reach a wall stile in the far left-hand corner. Cross the stile and follow the path as it ascends the shallow incline to the summit of Cunswick Fell, with its large cairn of limestones.

3 Head left from the cairn to reach a path taking you left again and southwards, adjacent to Scar Wood. Take care as you meet this path as there is a steep drop beyond to the woodland below. As you continue south, Scar Wood rises to border the path on the right. Continue on for 1,500 metres or so to reach a junction of paths at a wall return. Turn sharp left to reach a footpath sign to Boundary Bank after 100 metres. Follow the direction of this sign.

The path is poorly defined but the sign will guide you to a concrete stile set into the limestone walling. Cross and continue over the next field to another similar wall stile and, once over this, follow the wall on the left. After 100 metres, the line of the path bears slightly to the right and diagonally across the field to reach another wall stile next to the A591 dual carriageway. Carefully cross the road, making use of the grass central reservation, and continue into woodland on the other side.

4 At a junction of paths go left for a short distance and then right and through a gate onto an enclosed, signposted footpath. Pass through gates and continue uphill following the waymarks taking you diagonally left across a field to another gate. Turn right here and pass double field gates at a cattle grid (the narrow path is on the left) and along a country lane with woods on the right. The path takes a sharp left after 150 metres and then a right, past a small settlement. Once clear of the buildings you have the choice of continuing on the lane for 500 metres to reach the Underbarrow Road, turning left and continuing downhill to reach Queens Road.

5 The more interesting alternative indicated on the map is to follow the signage on the left at the end of the settlement buildings, crossing a stile and heading uphill to pass through a gate and into a field. Bear diagonally left across the field to a stile concealed behind a large tree in the left-hand corner. Negotiate the stile onto the right of way across Kendal Golf Course, skirting the green for a short distance to reach a waymark at the edge of woodland.

Follow the direction of the signage which takes you to the right and onto a waymarked path downhill next to the golf course, to reach another wood. Follow the sign directing you through the wood to emerge at a wide track, with an industrial storage shed on your left. Go left here and follow the track as it bears to the right taking you past the golf clubhouse and downhill towards a small village green. Head left, cutting across the grass to a gate in the far left-hand corner, where you will emerge onto Queens Road, and continue down the road and back to the starting point.

HEADING TOWARDS THE BARNS FROM HELSFELL NAB
(© Jumpy James)
www.jumpyjames.co.uk

Trail C7: Potter Tarn

Setting out from the Staveley Mill Yard, this hilly trail combines fell and road and passes Craggy Plantation, a densely wooded, publicly owned area of deciduous trees, and Potter Tarn, a small reservoir which supplies water to the James Cropper Paper Mill in Burneside. The tarn's flow is moderated by a concrete dam.

The start of this trail is accessible by both the 555 Stagecoach which travels between Kendal and Keswick, and the Lakes Line.

Approximate Distance:	7.5 km/4.75 miles.
Terrain:	Paths, grass and road.
Severity:	Some steep ascents and descents.
Approximate Time:	45-65 minutes.
Total Ascent:	241m.
Start of the Trail:	Park in the Mill Yard in the centre of Staveley village.
Map Reference:	NY 470 984 (OS Explorer Map OL7: South-Eastern Lakes – North Sheet)

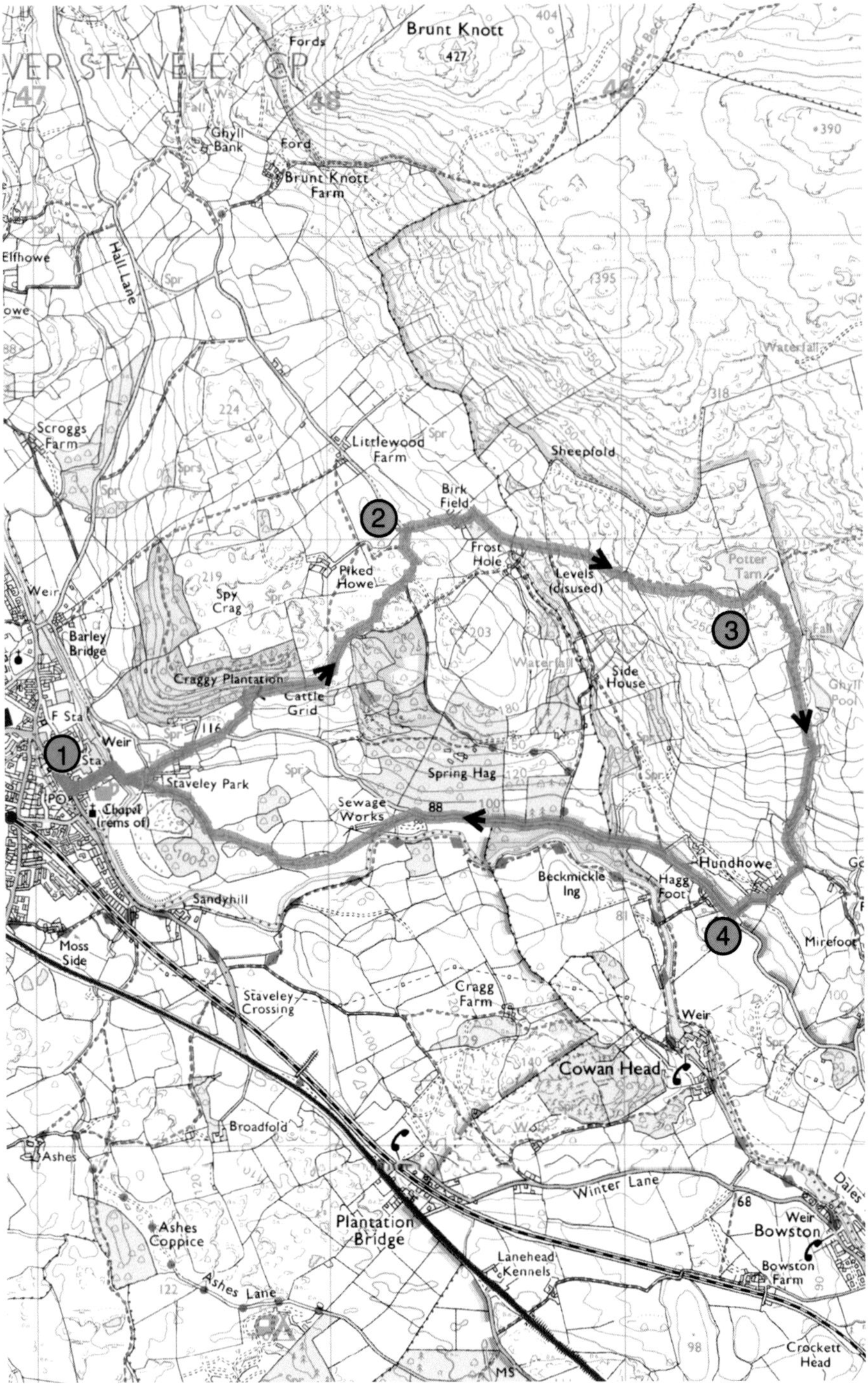
Brunt Knott
427
404
Fords
Ghyll Bank
Ford
Brunt Knott Farm
Elfhowe
Hall Lane
395
390
350
300
250
200
Waterfall
318
224
Scroggs Farm
Littlewood Farm
Sheepfold
Birk Field
Frost Hole
Levels (disused)
Potter Tarn
1
2
3
4
219
Spy Crag
Piked Howe
Weir
Barley Bridge
203
Craggy Plantation
Cattle Grid
Side House
Ghyll Pool
116
Spring Hag
Staveley Park
Sewage Works
88
Chapel (rems of)
Hundhowe
Beckmickle Ing
Hagg Foot
Sandyhill
81
Mirefoot
Moss Side
Staveley Crossing
Cragg Farm
129
140
Cowan Head
Broadfold
Ashes
Winter Lane
68
Plantation Bridge
Ashes Coppice
Ashes Lane
122
Lanehead Kennels
Bowston
Bowston Farm
98
Crockett Head

1 Turn left onto the main street as you leave the Mill Yard, and run past the supermarket, turning left again after a short distance onto the enclosed lane just before the tower of the former St Margaret's Chapel. This path takes you across the new pedestrian bridge over the River Kent. Turn right and through the gate on the other side of the bridge and then left at the wall return, following the waymark signage past former farm buildings.

Go straight ahead and up through the signposted wooden gate opposite, continuing uphill on the muddy path to reach a kissing gate adjacent to the entrance to Craggy House, on the back road to Burneside. Turn right and follow the road, taking a left at the next junction and continuing uphill as the road loops round the south and east sides of Craggy Plantation. At the top of the hill continue on the paved lane, ignoring the public footpath signs off to the right and left, until you reach the signpost to Potter Tarn on the right-hand side of the road.

2 Take this steep concrete path downhill to Birk Field Farm and head through the gate which leads you past the white farmhouse, through another field gate and then right through the next gate to follow a small beck along the bottom edge of the field. Bear left at the end of the field and head towards a wall gap and uphill to a gate in the right-hand corner. Once through this gate, turn right and then almost immediately left following the waymark signage for Potter Tarn.

Proceed diagonally uphill on the steep grassy path until you reach a wall gap. Bear right through the gap and then left though a metal field gate. Follow the isolated waymarks uphill over the field towards Potter Tarn. Looking back, you will see splendid views of the Central Lakeland Fells. Potter Tarn will appear on your left and the signage will guide you over a wall stile.

3 Head towards the dam and then bear right following the path downhill adjacent to Ghyll Beck. The path reaches a wall stile next to a metal gate. Cross the stile onto a farm track and head through two gateways, passing Ghyll Pool on the left. The path loops to the left, then right, into woodland adjacent to the beck. Continue on the steep downhill, and through a timber gate adjacent to a field gate.

The path eventually bears sharply to the left and in 100 metres or so look for a gate to the right which takes you on to a narrow, enclosed path, through another gate and into the farmyard at Low Hundhowe. Go straight ahead downhill, past some traditional farm buildings, through a metal gate and onto the concrete farm access track. The track passes the entrance to High Hundhowe, and continues down to the back road to Burneside.

4 Turn right and proceed along the road, past Hagg Foot Farm and Beckmickle Ing woodland on the left, until you reach the sewage works. Bear left at this point following the direction of the signage through a timber gate, and head along a muddy field to a wall stile. Negotiate the stile and head towards the pedestrian gate at the entrance to the flat meadow which fronts the River Kent.

Continue on the clear, grassy path across the meadow to another wall stile in the far right-hand corner. Once over the stile, follow the signage to the right and then bear left past a marshy area and a small tarn until you reach a field gate in the corner. This gate leads you onto an enclosed track which bears left and takes you through a metal gate, straight ahead onto a narrow path and back to the bridge over the Kent. Once over the bridge run past the slate office and retail buildings opposite the bowling green, and turn right into the Mill Yard.

THE DAM AT POTTER TARN
(© Jumpy James)
www.jumpyjames.co.uk

Trail C8: Orrest Head and Allen Knott

Orrest Head is arguably the most climbed fell in the Lake District where its modest height (239 metres) and urban location make it accessible to walkers and runners of almost every ability. The panoramic views from the top can be enjoyed after relatively little effort. The rolling countryside of the South Lakes on the northern fringes of the fell is a marked contrast to the colonised slopes and distant vistas of Lake Windermere and the central fells on the Windermere side.

Orrest Head was bequeathed for public use by the family of the distinguished local man Arthur Henry Heywood, on his death in 1901.

The start of this trail is accessible by 555 Stagecoach bus which travels between Kendal and Keswick, and the Lakes Line.

Approximate Distance:	7.5 km/4.75 miles.
Terrain:	Paved and constructed footpaths on the Windermere slopes, grassy paths on the trail to Allen Knott from the summit of Orrest Head, and short sections of road in between.
Severity:	A relatively steep climb to Orrest Head with a less steep descent through pasture on the north side, and fairly easy going thereafter. The trail skirts round the west side of the fell on the way back to Windermere.
Approximate Time:	40-55 minutes.
Total Ascent:	255m.
Start of the Trail:	The pay car park at Windermere Railway Station.
Map Reference:	NY 414 988 (OS Explorer Map OL7: South-Eastern Lakes – North Sheet)

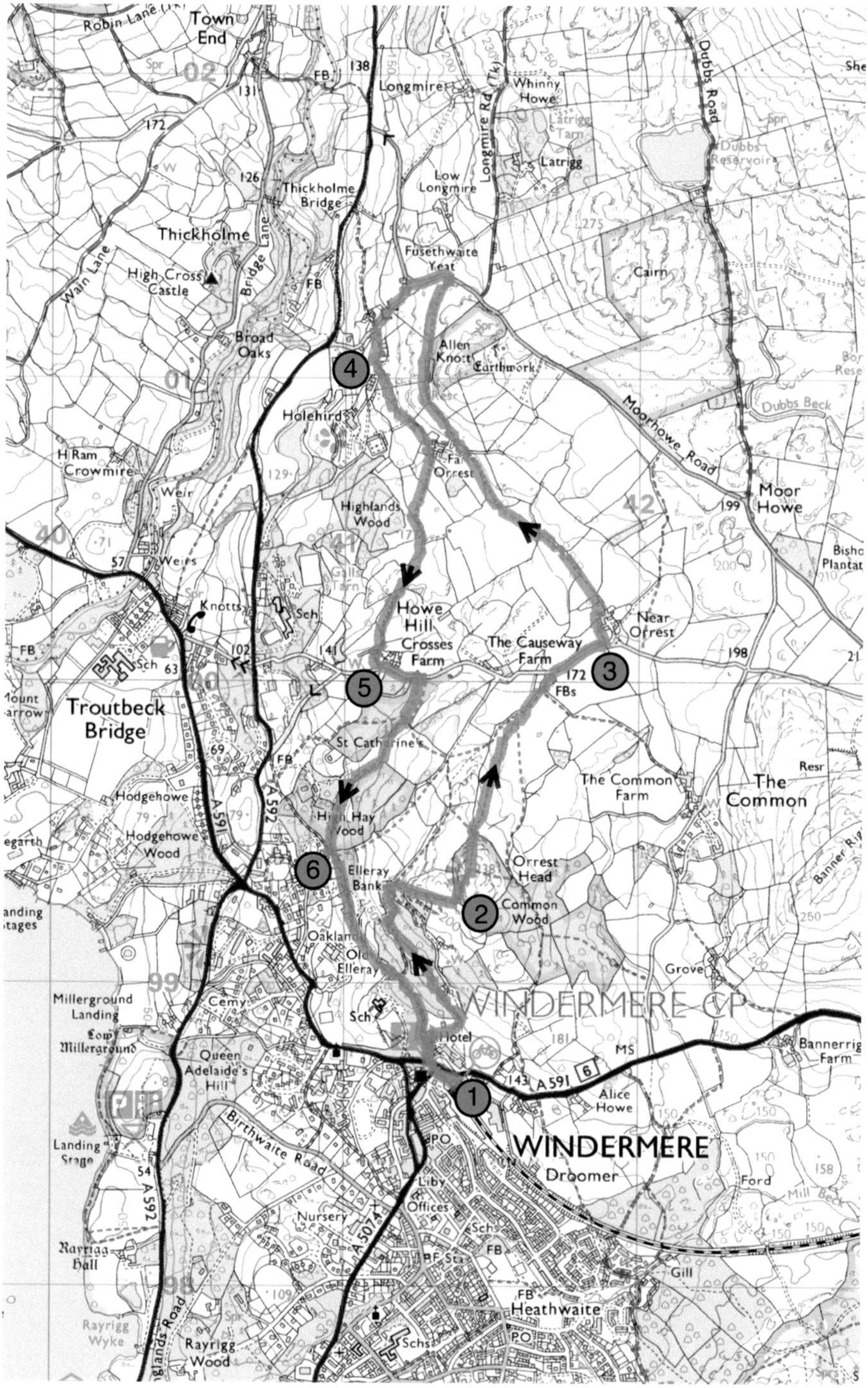
Town End
Thickholme
High Cross Castle
Broad Oaks
Longmire
Low Longmire
Whinny Howe
Latrigg
Dubbs Reservoir
Dubbs Road
Fusethwaite Yeat
Allen Knott
Earthwork
Holehird
Far Orrest
Highlands Wood
Moorhowe Road
Moor Howe
Howe Hill
Crosses Farm
The Causeway Farm
Near Orrest
Troutbeck Bridge
St Catherine's
High Hay Wood
The Common Farm
The Common
Orrest Head
Common Wood
Elleray Bank
Oakland
Old Elleray
Hodgehowe
Hodgehowe Wood
Millerground Landing
Queen Adelaide's Hill
WINDERMERE CP
Hotel
Alice Howe
Bannerrigg Farm
Birthwaite Road
WINDERMERE
Droomer
Grove
Heathwaite
Rayrigg Hall
Rayrigg Wood
Landing Stage
Nursery
Gill
Ford
Mill Beck
1
2
3
4
5
6

1 From the car park, jog carefully across the road into Windermere, to reach the pelican crossing over the A591, just beyond the bank on the corner. Take the signposted lane towards Orrest Head on the other side of the main road. Run up the paved lane, past the footpath junction to the left. As you ascend, the winding lane passes houses and several footpath signs leading to short cuts, which you should ignore, as you head up towards Elleray Bank.

When the paved surface peters out, continue on the main gravel path as it bears left and slightly downhill, and then returns uphill on a sharp right to reach a gateway. Here, the route turns into a more narrow, enclosed and winding path eventually heading west to east between a stone wall and a fenced off field. At the end of the straight you will encounter a metal kissing gate with memorial stones to Arthur Henry Heywood. Once through the gate head straight uphill on the uneven stone steps to the summit 50 metres beyond.

2 Enjoy the magnificent views before you descend the other side, slightly to the left of a stone bench. You should take care on the steep and potentially slippy grass path which takes you down to a stile in the wall corner, with a signpost for The Causeway. Cross the stile and continue downhill, keeping to the left-hand side of the pasture. The path levels out and becomes a rough track over a beck and on to a stile adjacent to a field gate. Go over the stile onto a paved country lane and turn right.

After approximately 250 metres, look for the stile signposted for 'Far Orrest ½ mile' on the left-hand side of the lane, just before Near Orrest.

3 Cross the stile into a field keeping to the right-hand side to reach a waymark at a kissing gate. Head diagonally across the next field to reach another gate into a copse, and pass through to a wall stile, which takes you into another open field. Continue straight ahead to a stile at a bend in the wall on the other side and cross to the next field. Stay on the right-hand side, passing a row of pollarded trees as you go, to reach another stile.

Cross the stile and follow the direction of the waymark, heading slightly to the right to pass through a wall gap. Carry on to a gate in the left-hand corner of the next field. Once through the gate go immediately right and through another gate, following the signage on a sharp left along the left-hand edge of the next field, parallel to an enclosed farm track.

At the left-hand corner the wall has been roughly rebuilt and the stile has been removed. Cross with care and continue on the left-hand side, skirting the base of the Iron Age hillfort of Allen Knott. Head through a wall gap and follow the direction of the signage taking you diagonally to the right to reach a metal field gate onto a paved country lane. Go left from here, following the left-hand fork where the main road takes a sharp right towards Troutbeck.

4 Head down this lane to a footpath signpost on the left, directing you towards Far Orrest Farm. Take this paved track over a cattle grid, past stone cottages on the left and fork left at an unmarked junction before some farm buildings, heading through open pasture to reach Far Orrest farm. Bear left at the buildings and then right, following the signage for 'Windermere via Crosses', and into the farmyard.

Turn right and then left, past the farmhouse, to a waymark at a gate into a field. Follow the farm track across two fields. Just before the end of the second field, turn left and follow the track with the wall on your right to reach a gate and wall stile in the right-hand field corner. Cross the next field to another gate and then follow the grassy farm track down to a metal field gate at Crosses Farm. Continue past the white cottage on the right to reach the country lane which you left at Near Orrest.

5 Turn left and follow the lane for 100 metres or so until you see a signpost for St Catherine's and Orrest Head, and National Trust land, at the woods on the right. Run through the woodland, cross a beck over a small wooden bridge, bear left at a junction of paths, and pass through a wooden gate into a field. Follow the path signposted for St Catherine's to the right.

Run towards the far corner of the field and turn right through a gate. Descend through the next field, with the wall and woods on your left. At the next junction of paths, carry straight on with a beck on your right and after 200 metres go through a wooden gate in the corner of the field and into woodland. Follow the waymarked path through the wood to reach a decorative iron gate.

6 Turn left here to follow the sign for Orrest Head and Windermere. Navigation is straightforward here as you carry on, ignoring paths off to left and right on the mostly enclosed path. When you reach the lane at Elleray Bank carry on with a field on the right and woods on the left. Continue past the access point for Windermere School, going straight ahead along the path next to a garage, and at the next junction turn right to rejoin the outgoing path, heading back to the A591 and the start of the run.

LOOKING NORTH TOWARDS ALLEN KNOTT FROM THE SUMMIT OF ORREST HEAD
(The Author)

THE FOOTBRIDGE IN ST CATHERINE'S ESTATE
(© Jumpy James)
www.jumpyjames.co.uk

Trail C9: Elf Howe and Littlewood Farm

This trail sets out from the layby at Barley Bridge as you leave Staveley, heading north on the Kentmere Road. The layby is often used by mountain bikers as they set out for Kentmere and beyond. Low Elf Howe is a farm on the east side of the road, which now mainly consists of holiday cottages. The trail takes in Littlewood Farm, with its restored slate barn, which is also partially converted to holiday accommodation.

The start of this trail is accessible by both the 555 Stagecoach which travels between Kendal and Keswick, and the Lakes Line.

Approximate Distance: 5.0 km/3.0 miles.

Terrain: Paths, grass and road.

Severity: Steep climbing on the road up to Elf Howe and Hall Lane, and a steep downhill over fields, back to Staveley.

Approximate Time: 25-40 minutes.

Total Ascent: 196m.

Start of the Trail: Park in the layby at Barley Bridge, north of Staveley, on the Kentmere Road.

Map Reference: NY 470 988 (OS Explorer Map OL7: South-Eastern Lakes – North Sheet)

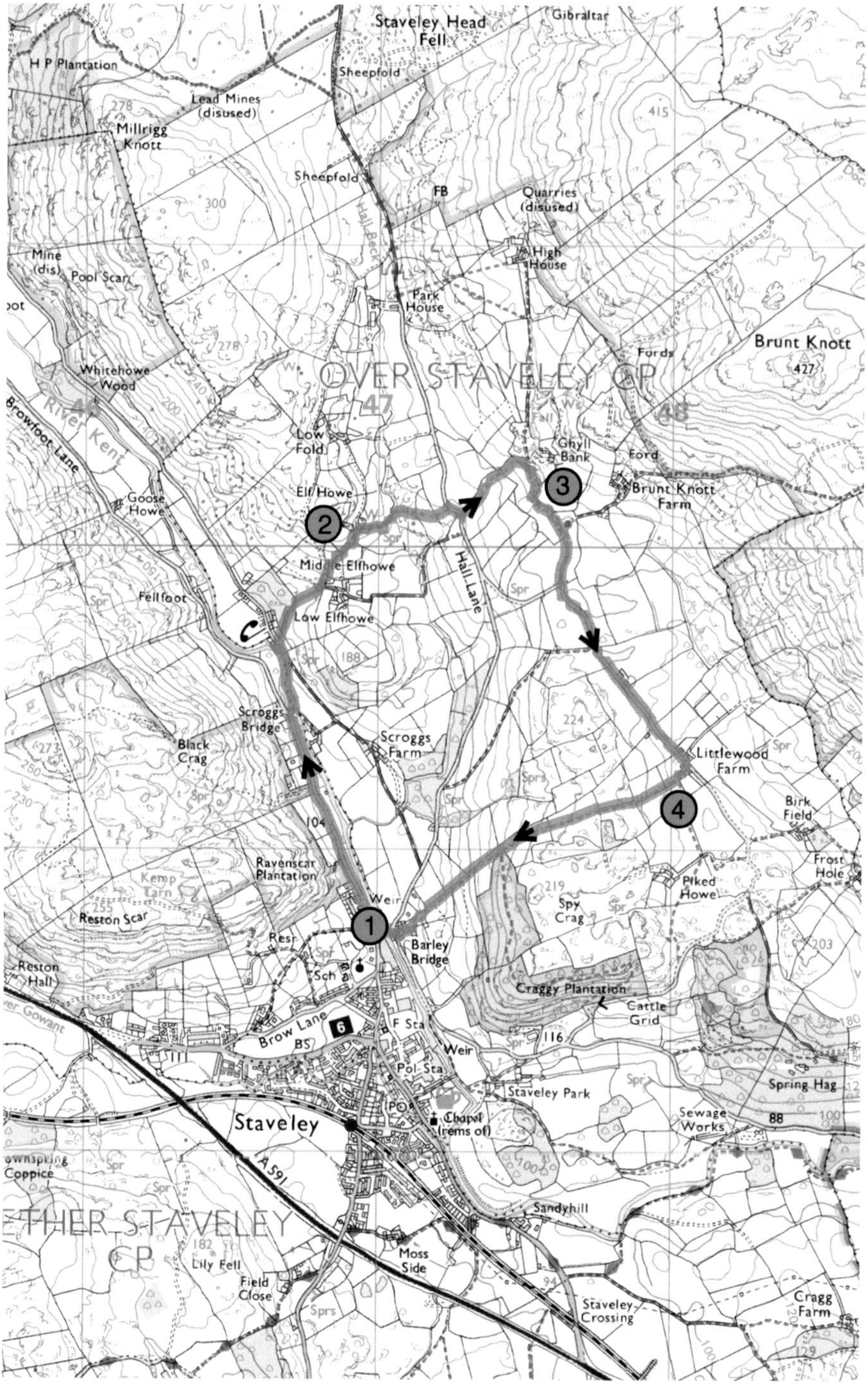
Staveley Head Fell
Gibraltar
H P Plantation
Sheepfold
Lead Mines (disused)
Millrigg Knott
415
Sheepfold
FB
Quarries (disused)
300
Hall Beck
Mine (dis)
Pool Scar
High House
Park House
Brunt Knott
427
Fords
278
Whitehowe Wood
OVER STAVELEY CP
47
48
Browfoot Lane
River Kent
Low Fold
Ghyll Bank
Ford
Brunt Knott Farm
Goose Howe
Elf Howe
2
3
Hall Lane
Middle Elfhowe
Fellfoot
Low Elfhowe
188
224
Scroggs Bridge
Black Crag
Scroggs Farm
Littlewood Farm
273
4
Birk Field
104
Ravenscar Plantation
Kemp Tarn
Frost Hole
Piked Howe
219
Spy Crag
Reston Scar
Weir
1
Resr
Barley Bridge
203
Reston Hall
Sch
Craggy Plantation
Cattle Grid
Brow Lane
BS
6
F Sta
116
Weir
Pol Sta
Staveley Park
Spring Hag
PO
Chapel (rems of)
Staveley
Sewage Works
88
A591
Sandyhill
NETHER STAVELEY CP
182
Lily Fell
Moss Side
Field Close
94
Staveley Crossing
Cragg Farm

1 Head out from the layby on the Kentmere Road, crossing Scroggs Bridge after about 800 metres. Turn left on the other side of the bridge and take the first paved lane on the right, signposted for Elf Howe[9]. This lane is very steep and requires patience, particularly at the beginning of the climb. As you near the top, look for the footpath signage on the left at a field gate, which points you uphill through gates and across fields until you reach the derelict buildings of a former farm.

2 Turn right through the gate and follow the path downhill, through another gate, and onto the walled former access track. Cross the bridge over Hall Beck and head through a wooded area and up to a field gate. Once through this gate, continue on the distinct path ahead through fields and across two stone stiles until you reach the paved Hall Lane. Turn right at the lane and, after crossing a small stone road bridge, look for the sign on the immediate left which directs you over a stile and uphill on the left-hand side of the field to a wooden stile next to Ghyll Bank.

3 Head to the right after the stile and continue onto the paved lane, passing the junction on the left to Brunt Knott Farm. Follow the lane to a T junction at a recently constructed timber barn, heading straight on here and continuing downhill to Littlewood Farm, where you will see the restored slate barn on the left-hand side of the road.

4 Turn right between the farm buildings and pass through a field gate and then a timber kissing gate into a field. Follow the signposted path uphill, staying close to the left-hand side of the field. The trail continues over the hill, crossing several stiles as you go, each one appearing in the distance as you negotiate the brow of the hill. From the top, with Craggy Plantation on your left, the path heads downhill on a very steep section of pasture, to reach the outskirts of Staveley. Continue through a further gate to reach the Burneside Road where you turn right, and then left across Barley Bridge and back to the layby.

LOOKING ACROSS TO BLACK CRAG ON THE DESCENT FROM LITTLEWOOD FARM
(Lois Blamire)

[9] Elf Howe is the name of the promontory to the north of the farms which are named as Low Elf Howe and Middle Elf Howe on the OS map.

Trail C10: Reston Scar

Reston Scar (255 metres) is a steep promontory overlooking Staveley from the north west. The trail sets out from Staveley Mill Yard on the Kentmere Road before heading up the steep, grassy ascent to the summit of Black Crag, across the high moorland to Reston Scar, and back downhill to the village.

The start of this trail is accessible by both the 555 Stagecoach which travels between Kendal and Keswick, and the Lakes Line.

Approximate Distance: 4.5 km/3.0 miles.

Terrain: Paths, grass and road.

Severity: Severe climbing to the first summit and a steep downhill towards the end of the run.

Approximate Time: 25-40 minutes.

Total Ascent: 217 m.

Start of the Trail: Park in the Mill Yard in the centre of Staveley village.

Map Reference: NY 470 984 (OS Explorer Map OL7: South-Eastern Lakes – North Sheet)

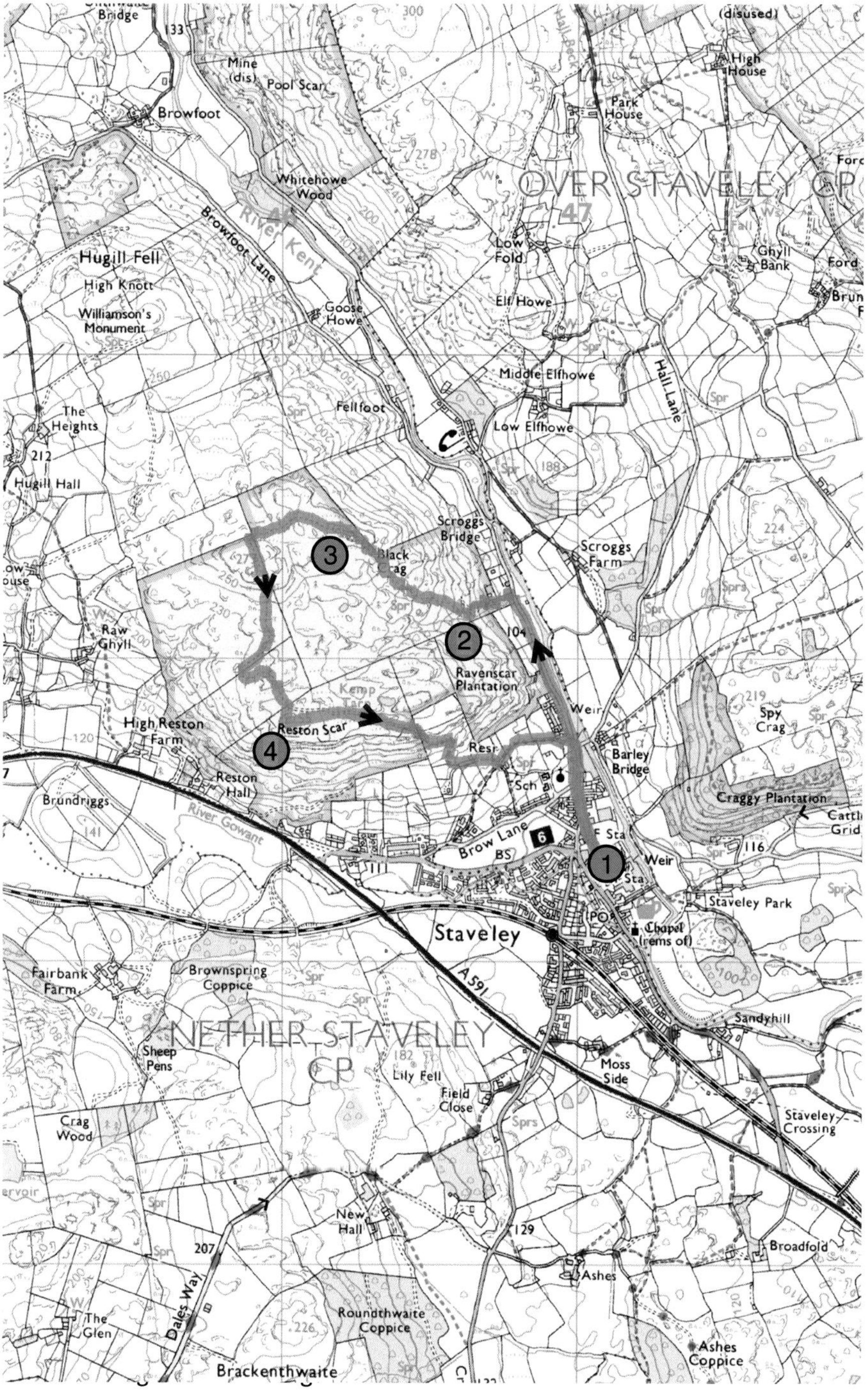
Bridge
133
Mine (dis)
Pool Scar
300
(disused)
High House
Park House
Browfoot
278
Whitehowe Wood
OVER STAVELEY CP
47
River Kent
Browfoot Lane
Low Fold
Ghyll Bank
Ford
Hugill Fell
High Knott
Williamson's Monument
Goose Howe
Elf Howe
Middle Elfhowe
Hall Lane
Fellfoot
The Heights
212
Low Elfhowe
188
Hugill Hall
224
Scroggs Bridge
Scroggs Farm
3
Black Crag
250
230
Raw Ghyll
2
104
Ravenscar Plantation
219
Spy Crag
Weir
High Reston Farm
Reston Scar
4
Resr
Barley Bridge
Reston Hall
Craggy Plantation
Cattle Grid
Brundriggs
141
River Gowan
Sch
Brow Lane
6
BS
1
F Sta
Weir
116
111
Staveley Park
PO
Chapel (rems of)
Staveley
A591
Fairbank Farm
Brownspring Coppice
Sandyhill
NETHER STAVELEY CP
Sheep Pens
182
Lily Fell
Moss Side
Field Close
94
Crag Wood
Staveley Crossing
New Hall
129
207
Dales Way
Broadfold
Ashes
The Glen
226
Roundthwaite Coppice
Ashes Coppice
Brackenthwaite

1 Turn right as you leave the Mill Yard, and head along Back Lane until it merges, after about 200 metres, onto the road travelling north towards Kentmere. After a further 800 metres, look for the public footpath which passes through a field gate on the left-hand side of the road. From here it travels steeply uphill, initially on a concrete track which provides access to a solar-panelled bungalow about 100 metres from the road. The concrete path turns to the right to serve the bungalow but proceed directly ahead and through a metal field gate.

2 You will now join a clear path which will guide you over the whole of the hilly section of the run. Pace yourself carefully on this section as the path meanders steeply uphill for approximately 400 metres, eventually reaching the angled wall return just below the summit of Black Crag. Continue on to the summit where you can enjoy panoramic views of Kentmere in the near distance, the Central Lakeland fells to the north west and the sea inlet at Arnside to the south. There is also a dramatic view down to the hamlet of Garth Row on the Kentmere Road, immediately below.

3 With the severe climbing behind you, continue on the path in a westerly direction to reach a kissing gate adjacent to a field gate. On the other side of the gate take the left-hand path and continue past an unnamed promontory on the narrow but distinct path. You will see Reston Scar in the distance but the path to it is indirect as it angles south west along a boundary wall for about 150 metres to another kissing gate next to a field gate. Go through the kissing gate and follow the path as it loops round to reach another field gate just below the summit of Reston Scar. Go through this gate and up to the cairn where you can continue to enjoy the panoramic views.

4 From Reston Scar head downhill, due east, towards Kemp Tarn. The path is less clearly defined at this point but loops slightly right before the tarn and, as it becomes more distinct, head towards a gap in the wall. Once through the gap take a sharp right and go through the next opening and onto a farm track which zigzags down towards Staveley. Pass through another field gate and past the stone building housing the Staveley Water Treatment Works, to reach the head of the paved lane up from Brow Lane.

Continue down this road for about 40 metres and turn left to reach a metal gate next to the entrance to Sunnybank. Go through the metal gate, and over a stone stile, and follow the enclosed path downhill through a timber gate and two further field gates to reach the Kentmere Road. Turn right and retrace your steps back to Back Lane and the Mill Yard.

RESTON SCAR FROM THE WINDERMERE ROAD IN STAVELEY
(The Author)

THE EAST

Trail E1: Orton

Historically, the pretty village of Orton was part of the county of Westmorland but it is now in the Eden District of Cumbria. It lies in open moorland about 15 miles south of the District's administrative centre of Penrith.

Orton is within the Yorkshire Dales National Park, which encompasses parts of Lancashire as well as Cumbria and North West Yorkshire. The trail incorporates short sections of Alfred Wainwright's Coast to Coast Walk which covers 182 miles from St Bees in Cumbria, on the Irish Sea, to the North Sea coast at Robin Hood's Bay, near Whitby in North Yorkshire. The trail consists primarily of open moorland and passes through some small farms, several of which have been converted into holiday cottages.

Orton has bus services from Kendal, Penrith, Appleby and Shap.

Approximate Distance: 7.5 km/4.75 miles.

Terrain: Grassy paths, tracks and short sections of road.

Severity: Easy, generally low level.

Approximate Time: 45-60 minutes.

Total Ascent: 185m.

Start of the Trail: From the centre of Kendal take the A685 north east, passing through Grayrigg and Tebay. Follow the sign for Orton at the roundabout immediately south of Old Tebay.

From the north, travel south on the M6 to Junction 39 at Shap, cross the motorway and turn left at the signpost for Orton, which is a further 4 miles south, on the B6261.

Park in the centre of Orton, adjacent to the Chocolate Factory.

Map Reference: NY 623 082 (OS Explorer Map OL19: Howgill Fells and Upper Eden Valley – South Sheet)

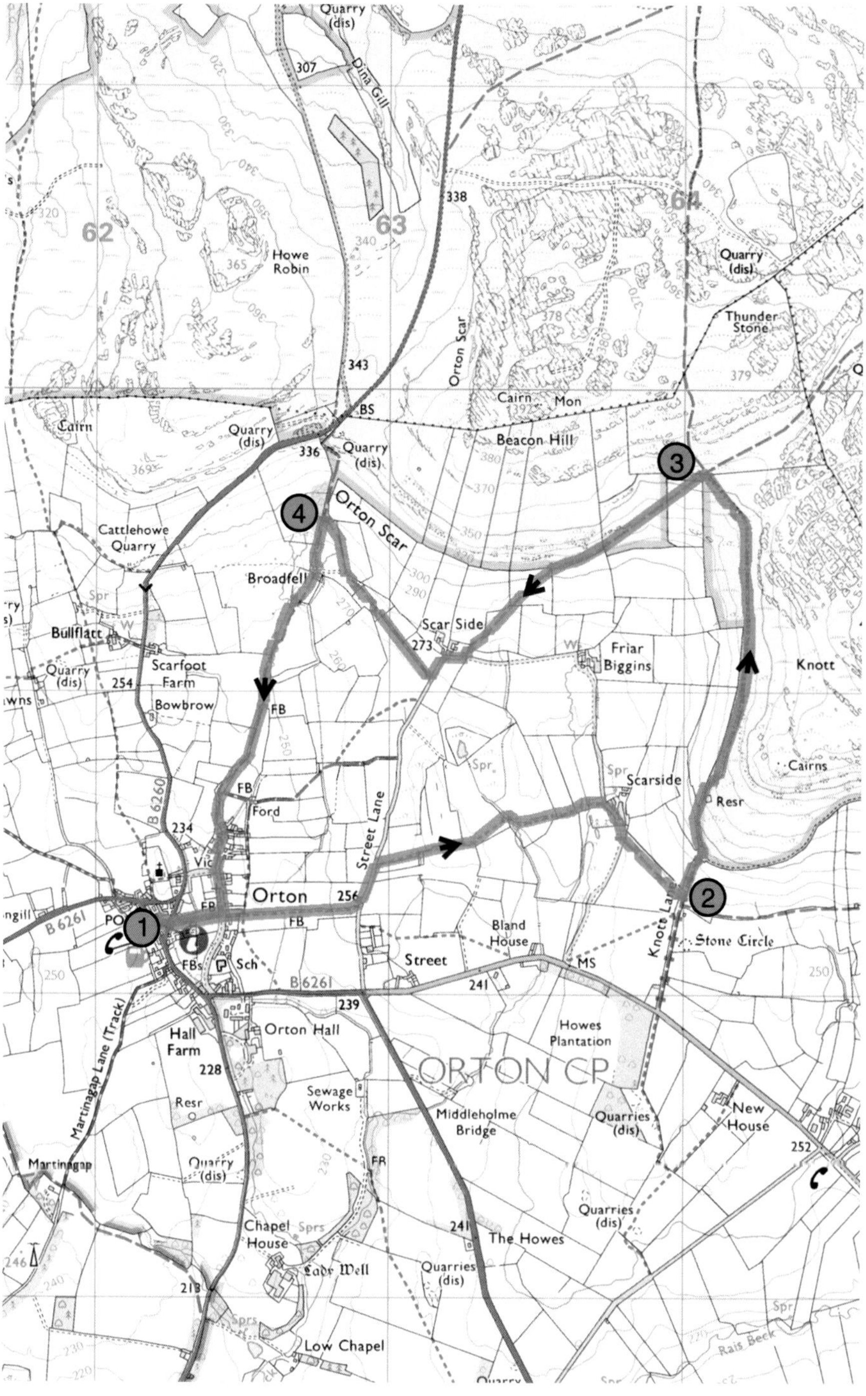
Quarry (dis)
307
Dina Gill
62
63
64
338
Howe Robin
365
Quarry (dis)
Thunder Stone
Orton Scar
378
379
343
Cairn
Mon
392
BS
Cairn
Quarry (dis)
336
Quarry (dis)
Beacon Hill
3
4
Orton Scar
Cattlehowe Quarry
Broadfell
Bullflatt
Scar Side
273
Friar Biggins
Knott
Quarry (dis)
254
Scarfoot Farm
Bowbrow
FB
Cairns
Scarside
Resr
FB
Ford
Street Lane
B 6260
234
Vic
Orton
256
2
Knott Lane
B 6261
PO
1
FB
FBs
Sch
Bland House
Stone Circle
Street
MS
241
B 6261
239
Hall Farm
Orton Hall
Howes Plantation
228
ORTON CP
Martinagap Lane (Track)
Resr
Sewage Works
Middleholme Bridge
Quarries (dis)
New House
252
Martinagap
Quarry (dis)
FB
Chapel House
241
The Howes
Quarries (dis)
246
Lady Well
Quarries (dis)
213
Low Chapel
Rais Beck

1 From the car park head directly east between buildings to reach the Appleby Road. Continue straight on past a bus shelter commemorating the Coronation of 1953 and take a footpath over a small footbridge to the right. Pass along the paved path as it continues east, next to a children's play area and school playing fields to reach another footbridge. Cross the road and go straight ahead onto an enclosed, signposted path for a short distance, to reach a gated stile onto open pasture. Stay to the left of the field, crossing another small footbridge to reach a gated stile onto the paved Street Lane.

Go left on the lane for 100 metres and look for the footpath sign to Scarside Farm[10] on the right-hand side. Continue directly east across muddy fields (ignoring the waymark at a pedestrian gate to the right-hand side of the field), passing through wall gaps to reach a gate into an enclosed field next to the farm. Carry on up to a field gate and turn right onto a paved lane. Beyond the farm buildings, look for a public bridleway sign on the left for 'Knott Lane ¼ of a mile' and the 'Coast to Coast Walk'. Continue across the field, parallel to the left-hand boundary, taking the direct line of the signage to reach Knott Lane.

2 Go through the gate and turn left onto Knott Lane. Over the wall to the right you will see the remains of the Gamelands Neolithic Stone Circle. Carry on up to the field gate at the end of the lane and turn left onto the open moorland below the National Nature Reserve of Great Asby Scar. Continue along the clear path with a wall on your left for 800 metres until you reach the wall return. From here the path continues diagonally left across open pasture to a wall return in the far-left corner. Pass through the gate to reach a four-way signpost.

3 From the signpost head sharp left for a short distance to a waymarked metal gate into a field. Continue following the waymarks at the gates and wall gaps between fields as you head along the pasture and diagonally down to the westmost Scar Side Farm. Follow the signs as you skirt left round the buildings onto a farm access track. Follow the track for a short distance to reach the north end of Street Lane. Go left on the lane for 50 metres to reach a footpath sign for the Coast to Coast walk on the right. Take this path and as you approach the small holding of Broadfell, head diagonally to the right to reach a copse of fir trees.

4 The path to the right at this point leads to the limestone pavements of Orton Scar but instead follow the footpath sign sharp left for Orton. Carry on into and across the yard at Broadfell, through a metal field gate and along a grassy path. The path continues through gates and across stiles, following the direction of Chapel Beck.

As the beck heads to the left after 800 metres continue southwards to the field gate welcoming you back into Orton, and run along an enclosed track to the road into the village. Cross a small road bridge and remain on the eastmost road into the village to reach the footbridge at the school playing fields. Turn right, cross the bridge, and return to the start of the run.

THE FOOTBRIDGE ON THE DEPARTURE FROM ORTON
(© Jumpy James)
www.jumpyjames.co.uk

[10] Scarside Farm should not be confused with Scar Side, which you will pass through later on the run.

Trail E2: Lowgill and the River Lune

This trail sets out from the Grade II listed Lowgill Viaduct which was built in 1859 by Joseph Locke and John Errington for the Ingleton Branch Line of the London and North Western Railway. The viaduct carried the railway over the valley of an unnamed tributary of the River Lune, south of the hamlet of Lowgill, where there was a railway station. The branch line closed in 1954 and the viaduct is now disused. It remains a distinctive local landmark which can be seen from the nearby M6 motorway.

The trail follows the reverse direction of the Dales Way (80 Miles between Ilkley in West Yorkshire and Bowness-on-Windermere) along the eastern bank of the River Lune, returning by fields, farms and meadows. Care should be taken during the summer when some of the fields are grazing land for cows with calves, particularly on the return journey between Beckside and Beck Foot farms. If you are concerned about this, there is an alternative return journey by paved lane.

Approximate Distance: 6.5 km/4.0 miles.

Terrain: A combination of fields, paths, farm tracks and paved country lanes.

Severity: Relatively mild in terms of ascent and descent along the River Lune and on the return journey from Beckside. However, some of the footpaths are not in regular use and may be difficult to follow from time to time, without prior investigation.

The alternative return journey on the paved lane has several steep inclines.

Approximate Time: 35-50 minutes.

Total Ascent: 197m.

Start of the Trail: Leave Kendal on the A684, heading towards Sedbergh. After approximately eight miles, look for the B6257 on the left-hand side of the road, just before Lincoln's Inn Bridge. Follow this road for about three miles, passing the Lune Viaduct, until you see the Lowgill Viaduct on your right. Park in the layby on the right hand of the road, near the junction of the minor road which passes under the viaduct.

Map Reference: NY 616 965 (OS Explorer Map OL19: Howgill Fells and Upper Eden Valley – South Sheet)

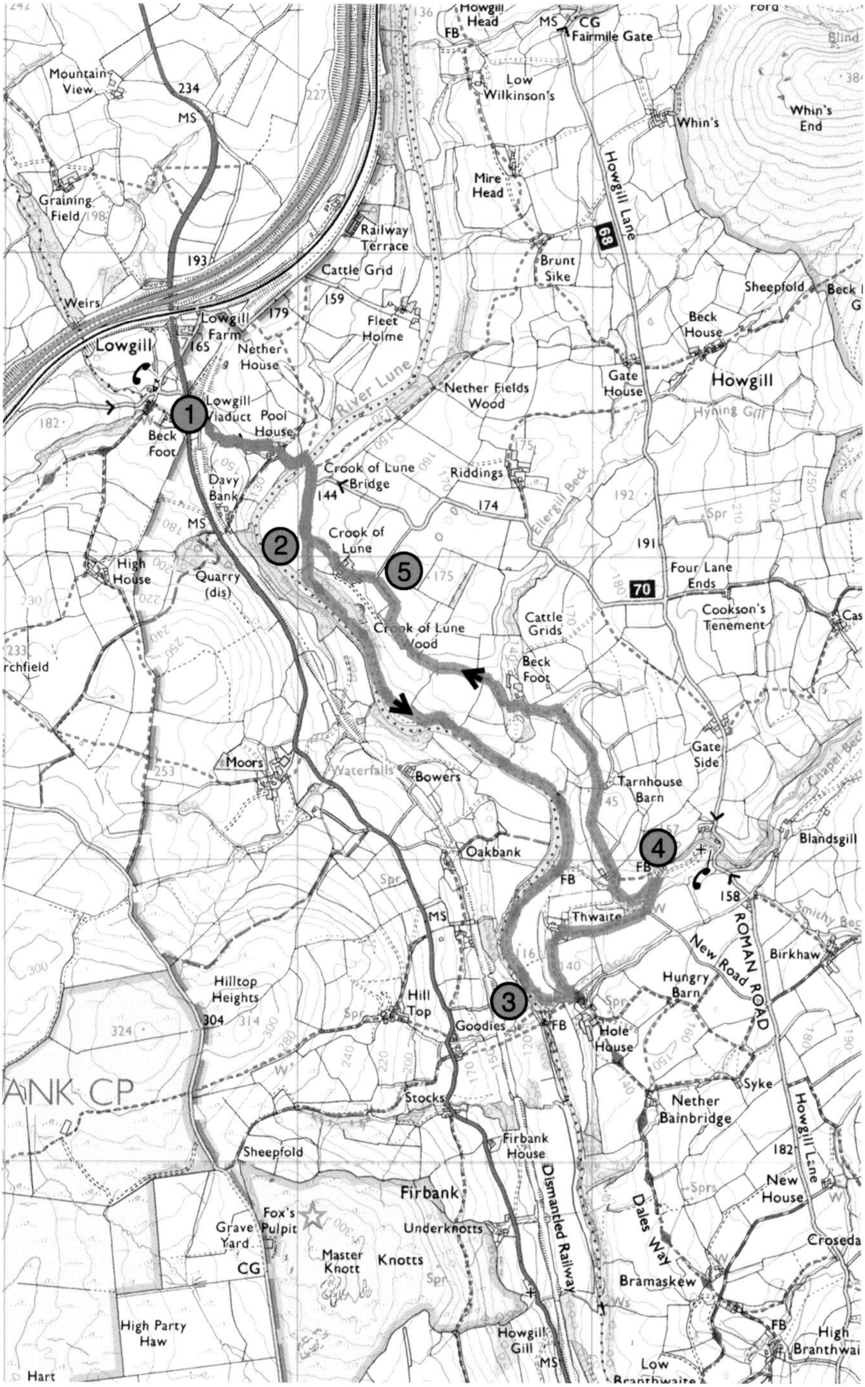
Howgill Head
FB
MS
CG
Fairmile Gate
Low Wilkinson's
Mountain View
234
MS
Whin's
Whin's End
Mire Head
Howgill Lane
68
Graining Field
198
Railway Terrace
Brunt Sike
193
Cattle Grid
159
Sheepfold
Weirs
Lowgill Farm
179
Fleet Holme
Beck House
Lowgill
165
Nether House
River Lune
Gate House
Howgill
1
Lowgill Viaduct
Pool House
Nether Fields Wood
Hyning Gill
182
Beck Foot
Crook of Lune Bridge
Riddings
Davy Bank
144
174
Ellergill Beck
192
MS
2
Crook of Lune
191
High House
Quarry (dis)
5
Four Lane Ends
70
Cookson's Tenement
230
Cattle Grids
Crook of Lune Wood
233
rchfield
Beck Foot
Gate Side
Moors
253
Waterfalls
Bowers
Tarnhouse Barn
45
4
Blandsgill
Oakbank
FB
FB
Spr
158
MS
Thwaite
ROMAN ROAD
New Road
Birkhaw
116
140
Hungry Barn
Hilltop Heights
Hill Top
3
Goodies
FB
Hole House
324
304
314
Syke
ANK CP
Stocks
Nether Bainbridge
Firbank House
Howgill Lane
Sheepfold
182
Dismantled Railway
Dales Way
New House
Firbank
Fox's Pulpit
Grave Yard
Underknotts
Croseda
Master Knott
Knotts
CG
Bramaskew
High Party Haw
Howgill Gill
FB
High Branthwai
MS
Low Branthwaite
Hart

1 Follow the Dales Way on the paved lane under the viaduct and head down to Pool House and Crook of Lune Bridge, ignoring the footpath sign on the right at the foot of the hill. Cross the road bridge and carry on for 50 metres or so to a stile and sign on the right-hand side, as the Dales Way leaves the lane and heads into fields alongside the River Lune. Shortly you will come to a junction of paths.

2 Carry straight on, following the trail down to a gate into Crook of Lune woods. Taking care at some steep and narrow sections of the path, follow the trail through the wooded area along the riverside, emerging onto meadow, and heading over small footbridges and through gates until you reach the junction of the river with Chapel Beck after a total of approximately two and a half kilometres. Cross the footbridge and continue on along the meadow at the edge of the river until you reach the junction with Smithy Beck. Bear left here and head up to the timber stile in the field corner.

3 Pass through and follow the path uphill to a sign where the Dales Way goes to the right and across a footbridge. Instead loop round to the left, ascending the very steep incline on the grassy embankment to the edge of the field above. Skirt round the field corner to the right and head for Thwaite Farm. Look for the timber stile at an arrow on the farm building on the right.

Negotiate the stile and turn left into the farmyard then right again and along the farm track to a cattle grid. Go left here onto a paved lane and down the steep hill to a junction at a settlement of holiday houses, with a church and old red telephone booth uphill to the right.

4 Take a sharp left and head downhill, crossing the stone bridge over Chapel Beck to reach Beckside Farm. Pass the right-hand side of the farmyard and head uphill and through a field gate onto a farm track which leads you to Tarnhouse Barn. Go through the gate[11] to the left of the barn and cross the next field diagonally, following the track downhill as it sweeps right and then left along the edge of the field to reach the footpath signs at Beck Foot Farm.

Follow the signage to the left of the buildings and descend to cross a small footbridge. Turn right and head along the side of Ellergill Beck, then veer left round a copse and along past waymark signage which directs you right and continues along the left-hand edge of the next field. Bear right across the field, following the waymark signage to a field gate. You will then be directed by the signage immediately right then left through a further gate. At this point head diagonally across the next field and round a wall return. Stay on the edge of the field with the wall on your left to reach a paved lane just before Crook of Lune Farm.

5 Turn left and follow the lane downhill and between the farm buildings to reach a metal field gate. Once through the gate you will shortly reach the junction of paths you passed on the outward journey. Bear right and retrace your steps on the Dales Way to the country lane, the Crook of Lune Bridge, up the incline and back to the start at the Lowgill Viaduct.

ALTERNATIVE ROUTE AFTER 3

Go right and up the less severe incline past the church and the red telephone booth to meet the main country lane. Go left here and up the hill to Gateside. Just beyond the buildings take a left through a field gate, and then right to follow the line of the indistinct public footpath through fields and across four timber stiles to re-emerge onto the lane.

Bear left and follow the lane past the offshoots to The Riddings, on the right, and Crook of Lune Farm, on the left, negotiating the steep inclines as you go. You will soon reach the footpath and stile you took on the outward journey, but continue on to the road bridge and up the steep hill to the viaduct and the start of the run.

THE LOWGILL VIADUCT LOOKING SOUTH EAST
(© Jumpy James)
www.jumpyjames.co.uk

[11] There is a sign next to the gate indicating that there is a bull in the field ahead.

Trail E3: Hutton Roof

This trail takes in a short section of the Limestone Link (13 miles between Arnside and Kirkby Lonsdale) heading through fields, past small farms with holiday cottages, and over open moorland. Hutton Roof Crags is a site of Special Scientific Interest, celebrated for its limestone pavements.

Approximate Distance:	7.5km/4.75 miles.
Terrain:	Paths, grass and some sections of paved country lane.
Severity:	A long, steady climb at the start of the run onto Hutton Roof Crags, and thereafter undulating terrain over fields and through farms.
Approximate Time:	40-60 minutes.
Total Ascent:	235m.
Start of the Trail:	From Plumgarth Roundabout to the north-west of Kendal, head south on the A590 dual carriageway, crossing the M6 after 8 miles, and carry on through the next roundabout, onto the A65 south to Skipton. Pass through Lupton and take the first junction on the right, signposted for Hutton Roof. Follow this undulating lane for 2 miles, to reach the village. There are several options for parking on laybys, all within a short jog of the starting point at the T junction in the centre of Hutton Roof.
Map Reference:	SD 571 784 (OS Explorer Map OL7: South-Eastern Lakes – South Sheet)

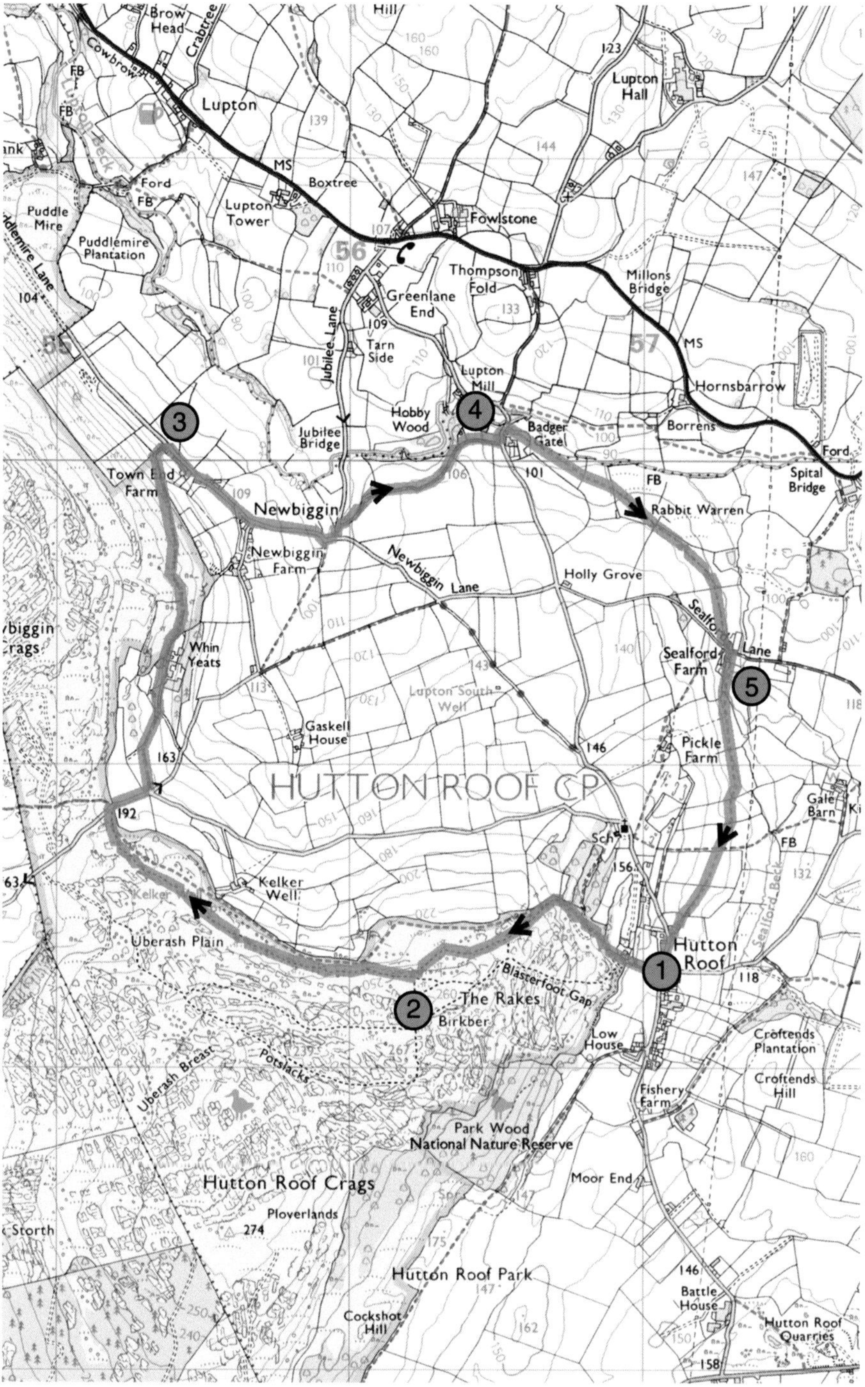
Lupton
Lupton Hall
Lupton Tower
Fowlstone
Thompson Fold
Greenlane End
Tarn Side
Jubilee Lane
Jubilee Bridge
Hobby Wood
Lupton Mill
Badger Gate
Millons Bridge
Hornsbarrow
Borrens
Spital Bridge
Puddle Mire
Puddlemire Plantation
Town End Farm
Newbiggin
Newbiggin Farm
Newbiggin Lane
Rabbit Warren
Holly Grove
Sealford Lane
Sealford Farm
Pickle Farm
Whin Yeats
Gaskell House
Lupton South Well
HUTTON ROOF CP
Kelker Well
Uberash Plain
The Rakes
Blasterfoot Gap
Hutton Roof
Low House
Fishery Farm
Croftends Plantation
Croftends Hill
Park Wood National Nature Reserve
Hutton Roof Crags
Ploverlands
Moor End
Hutton Roof Park
Cockshot Hill
Battle House
Hutton Roof Quarries
Uberash Breast
Potslacks
Gale Barn
1
2
3
4
5

1 From the junction head west up the farm track between houses, on the route of the Limestone Link, and through a gate guiding you towards Hutton Roof Crags. In a short distance there is a junction to the left but continue to the right on the main path and uphill to emerge onto a grassy incline which is bounded by bracken in the summer. The path eventually curves to the left to a junction on a promontory.

2 Take the right-hand path which heads downhill and becomes muddy as it enters woodland. Continue through and out of the woods to reach a kissing gate in the right-hand field corner. Turn right onto a paved country lane and head downhill for a short distance to reach a junction. Turn left onto the concrete farm access track to Whin Yeats Farm.

Carry on between the farm buildings to reach the farmhouse and take a left through a metal field gate. Turn immediately right onto a muddy path with a wall on the right, to a gate in the corner of the field. Continue on the wide grass path beyond the gate to reach a waymark at a farm track. Turn right onto the track and head down the incline to Town End Farm.

3 Bear right onto a paved lane, and right again, past Newbiggin Farm to a T junction. Newbiggin Lane ahead is signposted for Hutton Roof but go left here and then almost immediately right, through a gate onto an enclosed path between hedgerows. There are numerous waymarks on the path as it curves left and right, and down to the road at Badger Gate. Go left and downhill on the road for 50 metres, looking for a metal kissing gate and footpath sign to Sealford Lane on the right.

4 Once through the gate, follow the grass path and, as it turns to the right, look for the waymark at a small timber footbridge on the left. Cross the bridge and continue across the occasionally flooded fields. The footpath becomes less distinct as it takes you diagonally to the right to a waymark at field gates and on to a double wooden stile at a small beck.

Bear slightly to the right (some of the waymarks are obscured) and cross the moorland to another wooden stile and waymark. Go diagonally right and across the open field to another stile and waymark, and on to Sealford Farm. Cross the wooden stile onto a paved lane. Ignore the more obvious footpath on the other side of the lane, and turn left to reach another footpath sign pointing to the right, immediately beyond the farm.

5 Follow the direction of the sign, past the backs of houses and between parked cars and, although this area appears private, it is a right of way and you will shortly come to a reassuring waymark at another wooden stile. Head diagonally right and uphill through the field to another wooden stile with a waymark. As you cross the fields you will come to a junction of paths with waymarks for every direction and an obsolete wooden stile between open fields of sheep. Carry on to a metal field gate at a barn, and onto a stone chipped access track with houses to the

right, to reach a gate onto the road through Hutton Roof. Turn left and in a short distance you are back at the start of the run.

HEADING OUT ON THE LIMESTONE LINK FROM HUTTON ROOF
(The Author)

Trail E4: Dentdale from Sedbergh

Sedbergh is probably best known for Sedbergh School, an independent boarding school dating from 1525, which has been the alma mater for many public figures.

The trail sets out from the centre of the town and heads south, in the reverse direction of The Dales Way (80 miles from Ilkley, West Yorkshire, to Bowness-on-Windermere), to Brackensgill in Dentdale. It negotiates paved lanes and footpaths next to the rivers Dee and Rawthey, before skirting Sedbergh golf course and the playing fields of Sedbergh School, and returning to the town centre.

The start of this trail is accessible by the 502 Stagecoach bus which travels between Kendal and Sedbergh.

Approximate Distance:	8.5 km/5.25 miles.
Terrain:	Paths, fell and road.
Severity:	Undulating but not severe.
Approximate Time:	45 -60 minutes.
Total Ascent:	283m.
Start of the Trail:	Park in Sedbergh at the Information Centre and Pay Car Park at the east end of the main street which is a one-way street, heading east (the A684 from Kendal).
Map Reference:	SD 659 921 (OS Explorer Map OL19: Howgill Fells and Upper Eden Valley – South Sheet).

(The trail continues onto OS Explorer Map OL2: Yorkshire Dales Southern and Western Areas – West Sheet) for a short distance at the southern edge of the loop.

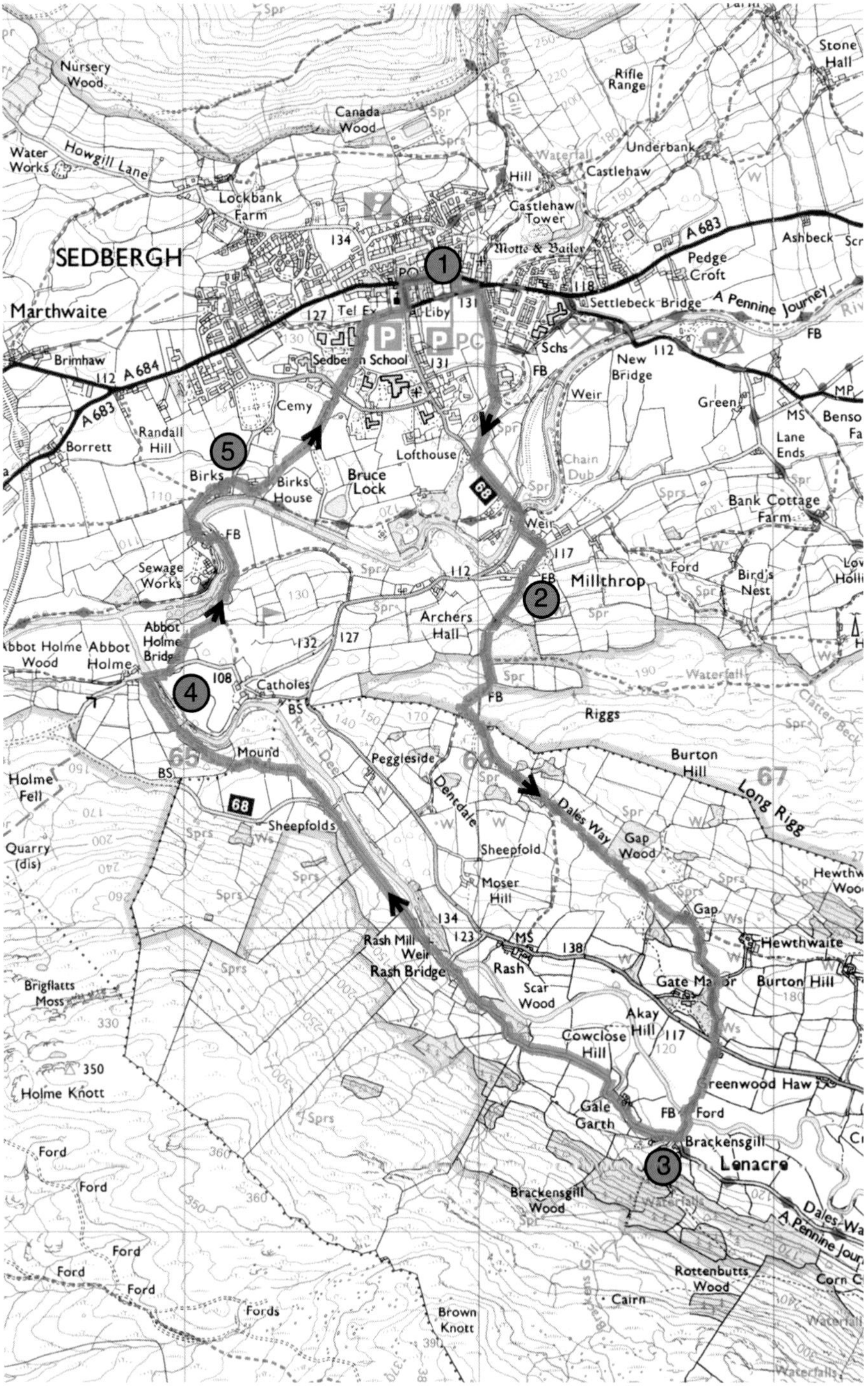
Nursery Wood
Canada Wood
Rifle Range
Stone Hall
Water Works
Howgill Lane
Underbank
Castlehaw
Hill
Lockbank Farm
Castlehaw Tower
SEDBERGH
134
Motte & Bailey
A 683
Ashbeck
Pedge Croft
1
PO
118
Marthwaite
Tel Ex
Liby
131
127
Settlebeck Bridge
A Pennine Journey
FB
Sedbergh School
Schs
New Bridge
112
Brimhaw
112 A 684
131
FB
Weir
Green
A 683
Cemy
Lane Ends
Borrett
Randall Hill
5
Lofthouse
Chain Dub
Birks
Birks House
Bruce Lock
68
Spr
Bank Cottage Farm
FB
Weir
117
Sewage Works
112
FB
Millthrop
2
Ford
Bird's Nest
130
Archers Hall
Abbot Holme Bridge
Abbot Holme Wood
Abbot Holme
132
127
108
Catholes
4
Waterfall
FB
Riggs
BS
River Dee
Burton Hill
Holme Fell
65
Mound
Peggleside
66
67
BS
Dentdale
Long Rigg
68
Dales Way
Sheepfolds
Quarry (dis)
Sheepfold
Gap Wood
Moser Hill
Hewthwaite Wood
Gap
134
Rash Mill
Weir
123
MS
138
Hewthwaite
Rash Bridge
Rash
Brigflatts Moss
Scar Wood
Gate Manor
Burton Hill
Akay Hill
117
Cowclose Hill
330
350
Holme Knott
Greenwood Haw
Gale Garth
FB
Ford
Brackensgill
3
Lenacre
Ford
Ford
Brackensgill Wood
Dales Way
A Pennine Journey
Waterfalls
Ford
Ford
Ford
Rottenbutts Wood
Corn
Cairn
Fords
Brown Knott
Brackens Gill
Waterfall
390

1 From the car park, head down onto the main street and turn left. Cross the road and take The Folly on the right, through to Back Lane. Turn left, cross the road, and look for the signpost to Millthrop, down Vicarage Lane. Go straight on through the metal kissing gate and uphill to another kissing gate at a lane. Cross the lane and pass through a further metal kissing gate on the far side.

Follow the clear path taking a right through a wall gap after 100 metres. Continue on the path diagonally left over the sloping field for approximately 200 metres to reach the Dent road into Sedbergh from the south. Go left, taking care on the potentially busy road, to cross the bridge over the River Rawthey. Head right and almost immediately left and continue on the paved lane to the pretty hamlet of Millthrop. Turn right at the T junction and continue on the lane between terraced stone houses.

2 As the houses end, look for the signposted footpath on the left for Frostrow Fell. Continue uphill on the rough farm track, through a gate and onto open moorland, as the track curves round the extreme western shoulder of the fell. Cross a small planked footbridge and head left at a fork in the paths to reach an isolated group of trees at a pedestrian gate in a wall.

Follow the Dales Way signage through the gate and stay next to the wall as it curves round to the left to a wooded area. Continue on the enclosed path between walls, and through gates and woodland to reach Gate Manor. Follow the sign for Brackensgill, continuing along the walled farm track and downhill to the Dent Road. Carefully cross the road and follow the clear, enclosed footpath on the other side and over the footbridge to reach Brackensgill.

3 Turn right onto the paved country lane passing the small Methodist Chapel at Gale Garth, to reach Rash Bridge over the River Dee. Do not cross the bridge but continue on the lane and, as it curves to the left after a further 600 metres, look for the signposted path on the right, with a stile and a sign for Abbot Holme. Cross the stile and follow the path over moorland, with a wall on the left, and down a grassy slope, to emerge at an isolated putting green on the Sedbergh Golf Course. Skirt the green on the right to a wall gap and onto the road at Abbot Holme. Turn right and cross the road bridge over the Dee.

4 Leave the road on the other side of the bridge, to follow the footpath sign for Birks, continuing across the meadow and a fairway of the golf course to a footpath sign at a gap in a hedge. Head to the left here on an unsigned path to reach a waymark at a gate. Once through the gate follow the high-level path on the right-hand side of the River Rawthey to reach the footbridge at a sewage works. At the other side of the bridge, turn right onto the paved lane and follow this as it curves to the right, next to the River Rawthey, to reach the hamlet of Birks, on the outskirts of Sedbergh. As the road out of Birks turns to the left, look for a footpath sign on the

5 right, at a kissing gate next to the entrance to Birks House. Go through the gate and, ignoring the offshoot onto the Dales Way on the right, follow the more distinct path as it curves round to the left, heading slightly uphill between the rugby pitches of Sedbergh School. Pass the recently completed Hirst Sports Centre to reach a road, and cross to the signposted footpath on other side.

Continue up and across the field, through a gate and between the buildings of the school. When you reach a junction of paved paths, go right along the path next to cricket pitch to emerge onto the Dent road. Turn left, heading up to the main street, and then right, continuing between shops for 150 metres to reach Joss Lane and the car park at the starting point.

THE FOOTBRIDGE ACROSS THE RIVER RAWTHEY ON THE RETURN JOURNEY TO SEDBERGH (The Author)

Trail E5: Winder

Sedbergh sits on the southern fringes of the Howgill Fells which stretch north for approximately 10 miles, to Tebay in the north-west and Ravenstonedale in the north-east. The fells of Winder and Crook, two grassy knolls about 500 metres in height, overlook the town from the north. The Dales High Way, which covers 90 miles from Saltaire in West Yorkshire to Appleby-in-Westmorland, and is not to be confused with the nearby Dales Way, dissects Winder and Crook and ascends from Sedbergh through Settlebeck Gill.

The trail is very similar to the terrain you might encounter in a short fell race. It is accessible by the 502 Stagecoach bus which travels between Kendal and Sedbergh.

Approximate Distance:	7.5 km/4.75 miles.
Terrain:	Paths, grass and short sections of road at the start and finish.
Severity:	Severe climbing on the grassy path to the summit, with a steep downhill on well-worn stony paths adjacent to Settlebeck Gill. Navigation is relatively easy.
Approximate Time:	40-60 minutes.
Total Ascent:	511m.
Start of the Trail:	Park in Sedbergh at the Information Centre and Car Park at the east end of the main street, which is a one-way street, heading east (the A684 from Kendal).
Map Reference:	SD 659 921 (OS Explorer Map OL19: Howgill Fells and Upper Eden Valley – South Sheet)

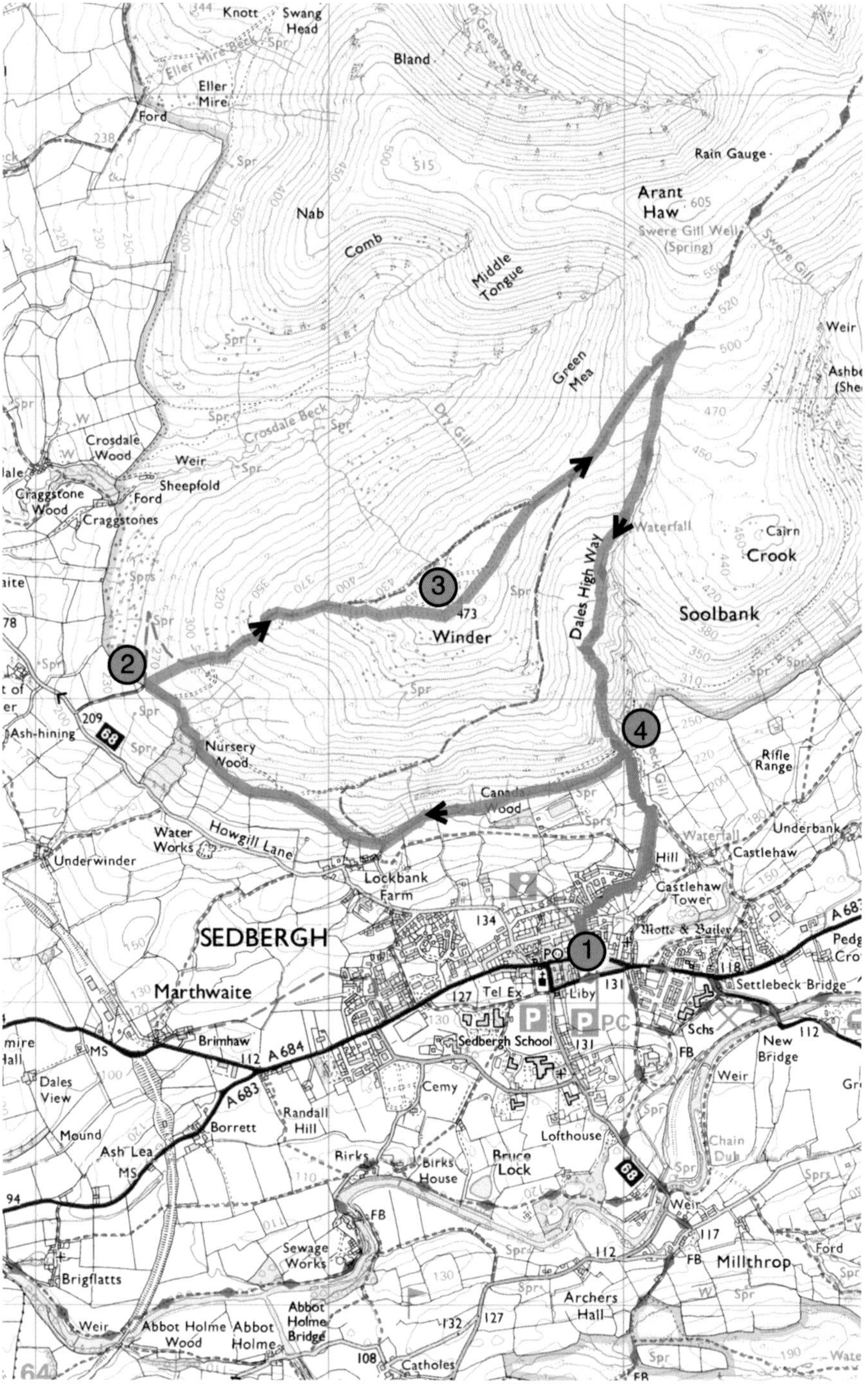
Knott
Swang Head
Bland
Eller Mire Beck
Eller Mire
Ford
Rain Gauge
Arant Haw
605
Swere Gill Well (Spring)
Nab
Comb
Middle Tongue
Green Mea
Crosdale Beck
Dry Gill
Crosdale Wood
Weir
Sheepfold
Craggstone Wood
Craggstones
Waterfall
Cairn
Crook
Soolbank
Dales High Way
473
Winder
Ash-hining
Nursery Wood
Canada Wood
Rifle Range
Water Works
Howgill Lane
Underwinder
Lockbank Farm
Underbank
Castlehaw
Castlehaw Tower
Motte & Bailey
SEDBERGH
Marthwaite
Tel Ex
Liby
Settlebeck Bridge
Sedbergh School
Schs
New Bridge
Brimhaw
A 684
A 683
Dales View
Mound
Ash Lea
Borrett
Randall Hill
Cemy
Lofthouse
Birks
Birks House
Bruce Lock
Chain Dub
Millthrop
Sewage Works
Brigflatts
Weir
Abbot Holme Wood
Abbot Holme
Abbot Holme Bridge
Archers Hall
Catholes
1
2
3
4
68

1 Head north up Joss Lane from the car park, looping to the right, and continuing through the gate at the top of the lane, onto a farm track through the lower fields. Carry on up and through the kissing gate onto the enclosed track alongside Settlebeck Gill. Pass through an intermediate gate and the top gate onto the open moor below Winder. Turn immediately left and follow the undulating path with the wall on your left, along open grazing land, passing to the north of Lockbank Farm after 800 metres. The path bears right, next to the wall, and crosses two small gullies at Nursery Wood before looping right and left, and heading down to meet the enclosed path up from Howgill Lane.

2 Turn right here on the open moorland and head uphill through the pasture on a path which becomes more clearly defined as you ascend. This is a steep climb, but your efforts will be assisted with a kind prevailing wind from the south west and comfortable underfoot conditions, taking you to the triangulation point and lookout pillar at the summit of Winder. Here you can enjoy the panoramic views of the Yorkshire Dales to the south and Arant Haw and the other Howgill Fells to the north.

3 From the summit of Winder, head north east towards Arant Haw, ignoring the several paths up from Settlebeck Gill until you reach the junction with the Dales High Way[12]. Turn sharp right onto the High Way and follow it in reverse as it descends steeply towards Sedbergh, initially on grassy paths which become stonier, and require care, as you approach the foot of the Gill.

4 Pass through the metal kissing gate and continue down the enclosed path you ascended on the outward journey. Go through the timber kissing gates and bear to the right until you reach the field gate at the top of Joss Lane. Head down the lane as it veers to the left, and return to the car park.

TRIANGULATION POINT AND LOOKOUT PILLAR ON THE SUMMIT OF WINDER
(© Jumpy James)
www.jumpyjames.co.uk

[12] You may be tempted at this point to include the summit of Arant Haw which is a short distance to the north, adding one kilometre overall to the run.

THE SOUTH

Trail S1: The Kendal to Hawes Bridge Loop

This trail incorporates short sections of urban as well as rural running, initially heading south from Kendal Leisure Centre on the Northern Reaches of the former Lancaster Canal. It follows the River Kent to Hawes Bridge, and returns through fields and meadow on the west side of the river.

The Northern Reaches (between Tewitfield Locks at Carnforth, and Kendal) became isolated from the rest of the canal following the construction of the M6 motorway in the 1960s and there is currently a campaign to reopen this section of the canal.

The start of this trail is accessible by several buses from Kendal Bus Station.

Approximate Distance:	6.5km/4.0 miles.
Terrain:	Paths, grass and some short sections of road.
Severity:	Generally level, easy going
Approximate Time:	35-50 minutes.
Total Ascent:	61m.
Start of the Trail:	The pay car park at Kendal Leisure Centre on the A65 Burton Road, Kendal LA9 7HX, which is to the south of the town centre.
Map Reference:	SD 520 914 (OS Explorer Map OL7: South-Eastern Lakes – North Sheet)

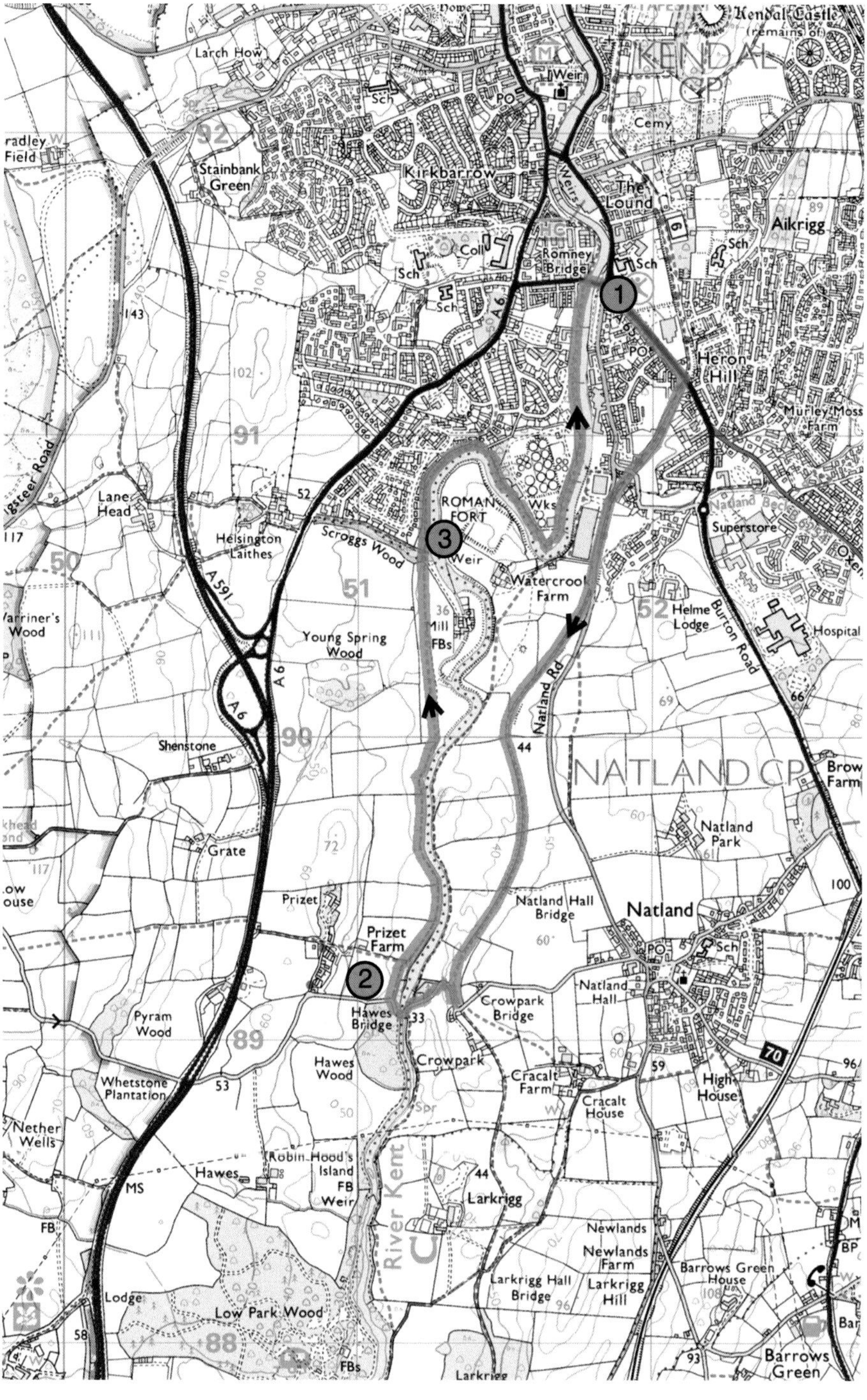
Kendal Castle
(remains of)
KENDAL
CP
Larch How
Sch
Po
Weir
Cemy
Stainbank
Green
Kirkbarrow
Weirs
The
Lound
Aikrigg
Coll
Romney
Bridge
Sch
Sch
Sch
1
Heron
Hill
Murley Moss
Farm
ROMAN
FORT
Wks
Lane
Head
Helsington
Laithes
Scroggs Wood
3
Weir
Watercrook
Farm
Superstore
Helme
Lodge
Burton Road
Hospital
A591
A6
Young Spring
Wood
Mill
FBs
Natland Rd
Shenstone
NATLAND CP
Grate
Natland
Park
Prizet
Natland Hall
Bridge
Natland
Prizet
Farm
2
Sch
Natland
Hall
Crowpark
Bridge
Hawes
Bridge
Pyram
Wood
Hawes
Wood
Crowpark
Cracalt
Farm
Cracalt
House
High
House
Whetstone
Plantation
Nether
Wells
Robin Hood's
Island
FB
Weir
Hawes
River Kent
Larkrigg
Newlands
Newlands
Farm
Larkrigg Hall
Bridge
Larkrigg
Hill
Barrows Green
House
Lodge
Low Park Wood
FBs
Barrows
Green

1 Cross Burton Road from the car park and head south for about 300 metres, turning off to the right at the signage next to the pedestrian crossing, and following the route of the former canal in the direction of Natland and the Lancaster Canal Trail. The trail soon reaches the Natland road. Continue along the road, passing the lane into Water Crook Farm and, after a further 100 metres, bear right onto the signposted footpath to Crow Park. This path follows the former canal along fields, over stiles and through gates, to reach Hawes Lane, just before Crow Park Bridge. Turn right onto the paved lane, winding downhill to Hawes Bridge.

2 Shortly after crossing the bridge take a right onto the footpath signed for Scroggs Lane. Continue on the clear path through fields next to the River Kent. Pass through a metal kissing gate and carry on through a further field to a wooden kissing gate. At this point take the left-hand fork diagonally across the field to a small timber footbridge. Follow the well-defined path across the next field to Scroggs Wood, pass through a timber gate and cross the road to follow the signage on the right, taking you into the east end of the wood.

3 Run along the path with houses on the left. At a junction in the path, take the right-hand fork down concrete steps to the riverside. The path follows the river as it loops round an industrial area and continues on to the busy road at Romney Bridge. Turn right to cross the bridge and continue on to the roundabout. Take the second road on the right, signed for the Leisure Centre, and return to the car park.

THE RIVERSIDE PATH TO ROMNEY BRIDGE
(Roger Blamire)

Trail S2: Crooklands and the Lancaster Canal

This trail starts from the small village of Crooklands on the Lancaster Canal. The canal was built in 1819, eventually closing to commerce in 1947. Much of it was drained and filled over the years, but the towpath is still used as a public right of way. In its 128-year working lifespan the canal, which has many bridges, now listed and protected, was the main artery for the import of coal and the export of limestone and slate, and manufactured goods including gunpowder. The canal waters on this trail remain extant.

Trail S1 outlines the campaign to reopen this section of the original canal, reconnecting it to the main stretch south from Tewitfield Locks.

Approximate Distance: 7.5 km/4.75 miles.

Terrain: Paths, grass and road.

Severity: Generally easy with short climbs on the paved byway and country lane after leaving the canal.

Approximate Time: 35-50 minutes.

Total Ascent: 88m.

Start of the Trail: From Plumgarth Roundabout to the northwest of Kendal, drive south on the A591 dual carriageway bypassing Kendal. Continue past the roundabout at the junction with the M6 and turn left at the next roundabout. Carry on for the short distance to Crooklands and take the road to the left, signposted for Milton. Cross Crooklands Bridge, turn sharp right and immediately park in the layby on the right-hand side of the road, adjacent to the small boating hut on the canal.

Map Reference: SD 534 836 (OS Explorer Map OL7: South-Eastern Lakes – South Sheet).

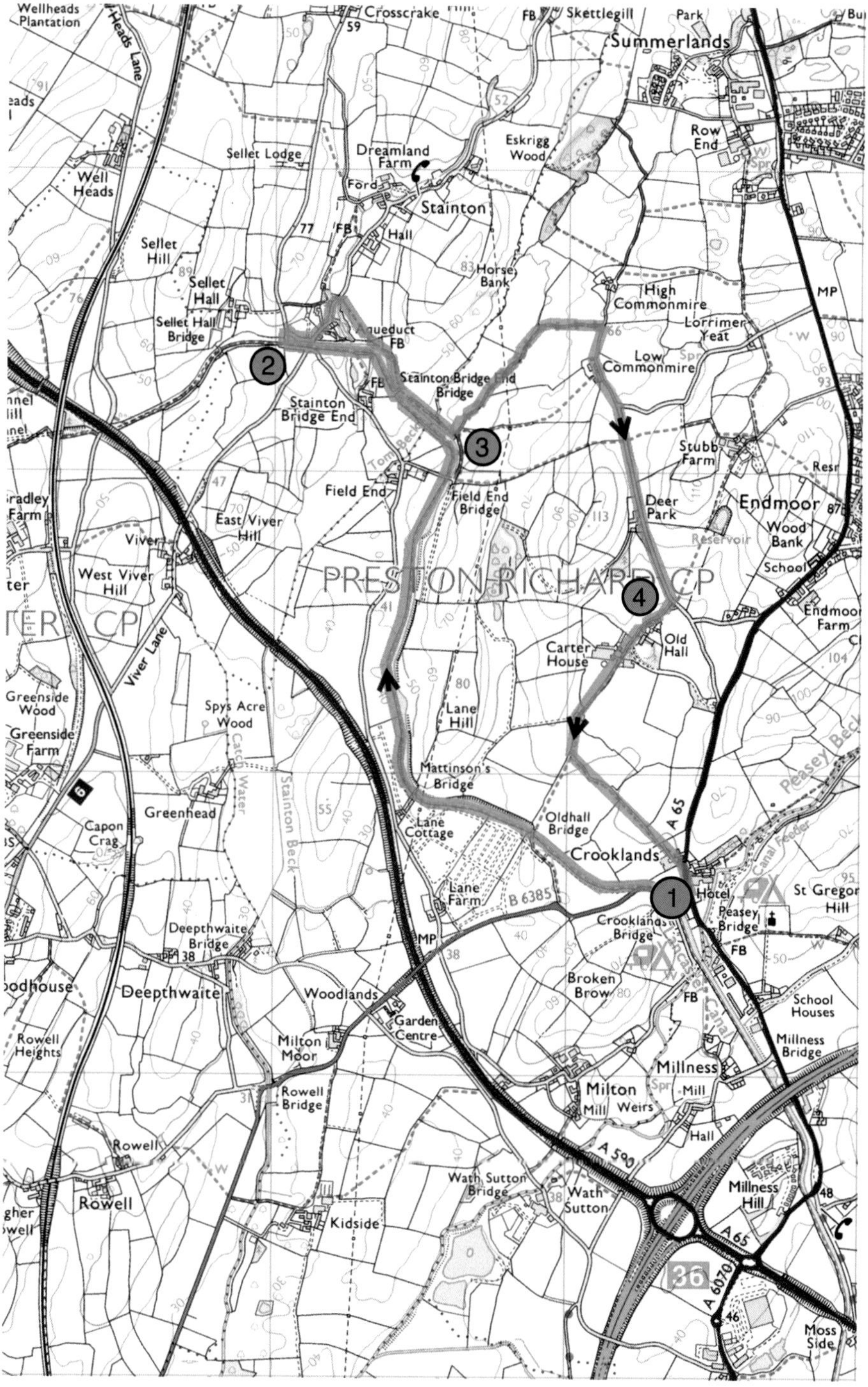

Wellheads Plantation
Crosscrake
Skettlegill
Park
Summerlands
Sellet Lodge
Dreamland Farm
Ford
Eskrigg Wood
Row End
Well Heads
Stainton
Hall
Sellet Hill
Horse Bank
Sellet Hall
Sellet Hall Bridge
Aqueduct FB
High Commonmire
Lorrimer Yeat
Low Commonmire
Stainton Bridge End Bridge
Stainton Bridge End
Stubb Farm
Field End
Field End Bridge
Deer Park
Endmoor
Wood Bank
Reservoir
School
East Viver Hill
Viver
West Viver Hill
PRESTON RICHARD CP
Endmoor Farm
Carter House
Old Hall
Viver Lane
Greenside Wood
Greenside Farm
Spys Acre Wood
Lane Hill
Mattinson's Bridge
Greenhead
Capon Crag
Oldhall Bridge
Crooklands
Lane Cottage
Lane Farm
B 6385
Hotel
St Gregor Hill
Peasey Bridge
Crooklands Bridge
Deepthwaite Bridge
Deepthwaite
Broken Brow
Woodlands
School Houses
Garden Centre
Milton Moor
Rowell Heights
Millness Bridge
Millness
Rowell Bridge
Milton
Mill
Weirs
Hall
Rowell
A 590
Wath Sutton Bridge
Wath Sutton
Millness Hill
Kidside
A 65
A 6070
Moss Side
Peasey Beck
Canal Feeder
Stainton Beck
Catch Water
Tom Beck
1
2
3
4

1 Go through the gap in the wall to the right of the hut, to start the run. Head left and northwest along the canal towpath passing under Oldhall Bridge (167), Mattinson's Bridge (168), Field End Bridge (169), Stainton Bridge End Bridge (170), and past the reconstructed aqueduct (171), to reach Stainton End Bridge (172).

2 Ascend the steps to the left and turn right, onto the paved country lane taking you across the bridge. Turn right again in a few metres onto the lane heading north east towards the village of Stainton. Cross a road bridge in approximately 250 metres and immediately take a right over a stile, following the signage for Commonmire Lane. Cross the field diagonally on the clear path to enter woodland on the east side of the canal, emerging onto another field in a short distance, and passing Stainton Bridge End Bridge. Follow the path along the field to another stile and through further woodland to reach Commonmire Lane.

3 Turn sharp left onto this paved byway, passing a footpath sign on the right, and head uphill between hedgerows to reach a T junction. Turn right at the junction and continue southwards on the lane past Low Commonmire and up and over the hill past Deer Park, until you reach the junction to the right, signposted for Crooklands.

4 Run along this lane and continue through Old Hall and past Carter House on the right, taking the preferred route to the left to avoid the farmyard, and carrying on to the sign in the field corner which directs you back to Crooklands[13]. Follow this route to the farm buildings and onto the A65, and jog down the pavement to the road bridge and back to the starting point.

LOOKING BACK ALONG THE CANAL TOWPATH FROM STAINTON END BRIDGE
(© Jumpy James)
www.jumpyjames.co.uk

[13]Alternatively, you can continue straight on at this point, taking you on the short distance through to Oldhall Bridge, to turn left along the canal towpath, and back to the layby.

Trail S3: The Sedgwick to Natland Loop

This trail starts from Force Bridge over the River Kent, near the village of Sedgwick, south of Kendal. It follows pleasant paths through fields and woods along the banks of the Kent, returning by the route of the former Lancaster Canal. The canal towpath is still used as a public right of way.

The introductions to Trails S1 and S2 provide further information on the canal.

Approximate Distance:	7.5 km/4.75 miles.
Terrain:	Paths, grass and road, with a relatively large number of gates to negotiate.
Severity:	Mostly level, with only slight inclines, throughout.
Approximate Time:	35-50 minutes.
Total Ascent:	118m.
Start of the Trail:	From Plumgarth Roundabout to the northwest of Kendal, drive south on the A591 dual carriageway bypassing Kendal and come off at the junction signposted for Barrow, just beyond the Low Sizergh Barn Farm Shop. At the roundabout take the first left east to Sedgwick and travel for about quarter of a mile, parking in the layby on the left, just before the road turns left to cross the River Kent.
Map Reference:	SD 507 868 (OS Explorer Map OL7: South-Eastern Lakes – South Sheet).

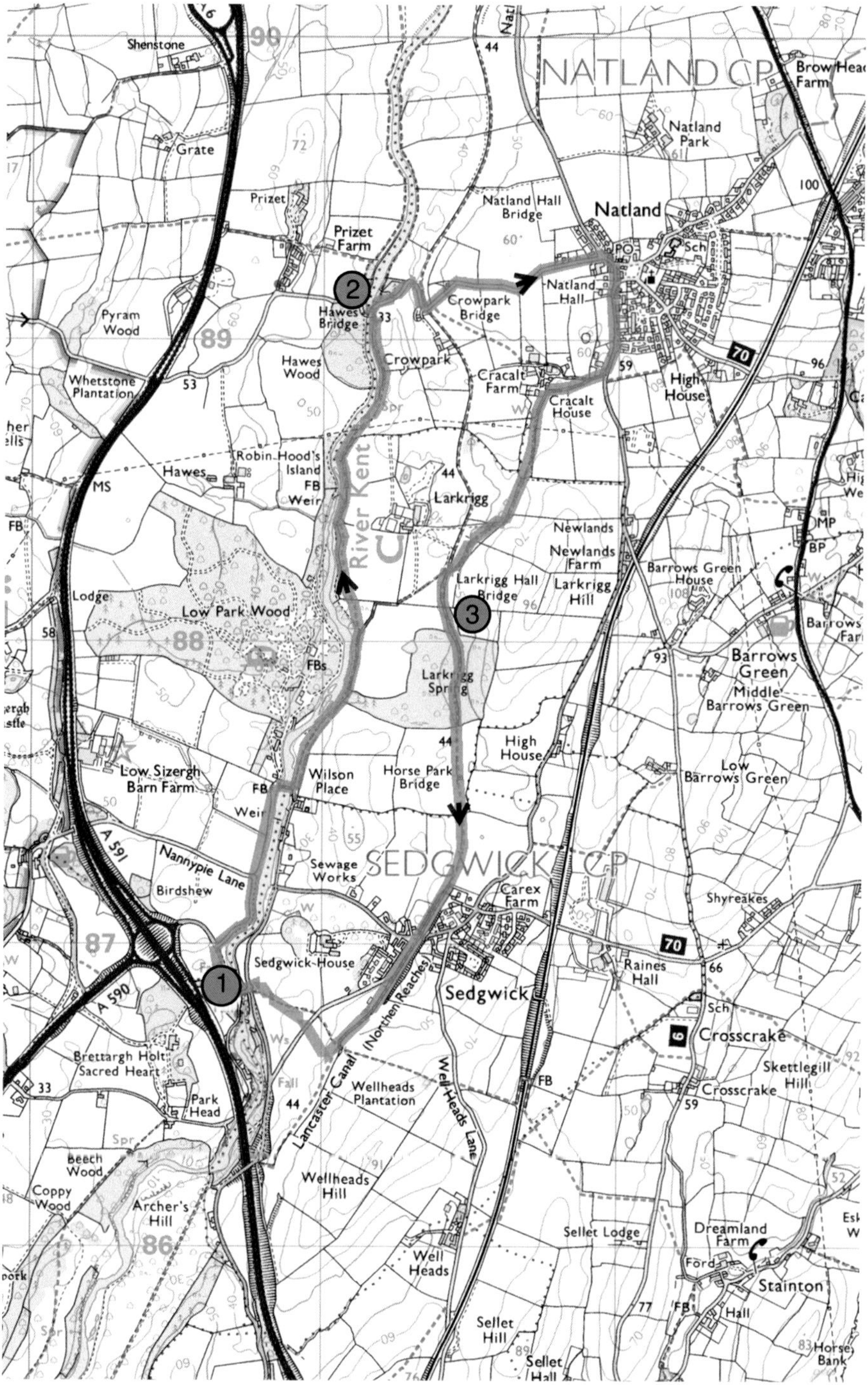

NATLAND CP
Natland
Natland Park
Natland Hall Bridge
Natland Hall
Crowpark Bridge
Crowpark
Cracalt Farm
Cracalt House
High House
Hawes Bridge
Hawes Wood
Prizet
Prizet Farm
Shenstone
Grate
Pyram Wood
Whetstone Plantation
Hawes
Robin Hood's Island
River Kent
Larkrigg
Newlands
Newlands Farm
Larkrigg Hall Bridge
Larkrigg Hill
Barrows Green House
Low Park Wood
Larkrigg Spring
Barrows Green
Middle Barrows Green
High House
Low Barrows Green
Wilson Place
Horse Park Bridge
Low Sizergh Barn Farm
Nannypie Lane
Birdshew
Sewage Works
SEDGWICK CP
Carex Farm
Shyreakes
Sedgwick House
Sedgwick
Raines Hall
Crosscrake
Skettlegill Hill
Brettargh Holt Sacred Heart
Park Head
Lancaster Canal (Northern Reaches)
Wellheads Plantation
Well Heads Lane
Beech Wood
Coppy Wood
Archer's Hill
Wellheads Hill
Sellet Lodge
Dreamland Farm
Stainton
Well Heads
Sellet Hill
Sellet Hall
Hall
A 591
A 590
1
2
3

1 Set out from the layby, running back on the road towards the dual carriageway. Take the first road on the right and continue on, ignoring the road to the left which is signposted for the farm shop. In a further 300 metres you will come to a footbridge over the Kent, signposted to Wilson Place. Cross the bridge and turn left onto a grassy meadow, following the clearly defined path towards the wooded Larkrigg Spring. Once through the field gate run along the path with a fence to your right. At the footpath sign bear left through a copse to a timber stile.

With a field on the right, go along the wooded edge of the river. Take care not to trip, especially in the autumn when fallen leaves conceal some stony ground and tree roots, and continue over the next timber stile. Looking left you will see some dramatic rock formations as the Kent heads downstream in the opposite direction. Once out of the woods, carry on to a decorative metal gate and turn right to enter another grassy meadow, with the river now much more tranquil, taking you in the general direction of the white painted elevation of Crowpark House in the near distance. Pass through a wooden gate and remain on the path through the field as it veers away from Crowpark, heading downhill, through another wooden gate, and onto the paved lane at Hawes Bridge.

2 Do not cross the bridge but instead turn right and follow the lane uphill, ignoring the footpath sign on the left, to Kendal, and carrying on past further signage until you reach Crow Park Bridge. Once over the bridge avoid the temptation to take the shorter route over the wall stile on the right onto the old canal towpath. Instead, continue on the road until you reach the village of Natland.

Turn right at the junction, onto the road to Sedgwick, heading out of Natland along a separate footpath on the right-hand side of the road. After rejoining the road, you will shortly reach a small intersection just beyond Apple Tree School, where you turn right onto the lane towards Cracalt House. After about 50 metres, take the left-hand fork and continue on the lane until the next junction where you turn sharp left onto a bridleway adjacent to farm buildings. Go through a metal gate and into a field.

The path blends onto a short section of paved track and in a short distance take the sign-posted bridleway on the left which leads you to Larkrigg Hall Bridge. Go over the bridge and turn immediately left and then right, onto the canal towpath, where the shape of the former canal is now quite distinct.

3 Continue on through a kissing gate into Larkrigg Spring. At the end of the woods go through another gate and onto a meadow, where the form of the canal is no longer evident, and pass under an isolated canal bridge, heading towards a kissing gate. Now you will hear the sounds of traffic on the A591 dual carriageway and may see trains heading to and from nearby Oxenholme Station. At the end of the fields go through the gap in the fence and a metal pedestrian gate onto a more clearly defined canal towpath, passing the rear gardens of private ground in the village of Sedgwick.

You will soon come to the Aqueduct at Sedgwick with the road through the village passing below. Here, the canal itself becomes much more apparent. Carry on for 500 metres, passing under the next canal bridge, and turn immediately right and up a short incline until you see the distinct trail head down over a field, crossing the road from the south into Sedgwick, and over a further field to a stile at the road bridge adjacent to the starting point.

CROSSING THE PEDESTRIAN BRIDGE AT WILSON PLACE
(© Jumpy James)
www.jumpyjames.co.uk

Trail S4: The Levens Park Loop

Levens Park was initially laid out by Guillaume Beaumont between 1694 and 1710, on behalf of the Bagot family, who owned the adjacent Levens Hall, a country seat which is Elizabethan in appearance and has a notable garden with exotic topiary. The park itself is bisected by the River Kent, and is well provided with fine trees, notably the 'Oak Avenue'. Deer, goats and sheep can be seen grazing in the park.

The trail negotiates its way through the park, heading downhill on the western edge of the river, and returning on the other side.

Approximate Distance:	4.75 km/3.0 miles.
Terrain:	Paths, grass and road
Severity:	Mixed, with a steady downhill path on grass on the west side of the river and a relatively long uphill section on the east side.
Approximate Time:	25-40 minutes.
Total Ascent:	80m.
Start of the Trail:	From Plumgarth Roundabout to the northwest of Kendal, drive south on the A590 dual carriageway bypassing Kendal and come off at the roundabout signposted for Barrow. From the roundabout take the first left east to Sedgwick and travel for about quarter of a mile, parking in the layby on the left, just before the road turns left to cross the River Kent.
Map Reference:	SD 507 868 (OS Explorer Map OL7 – South-Eastern Lakes: South Sheet).

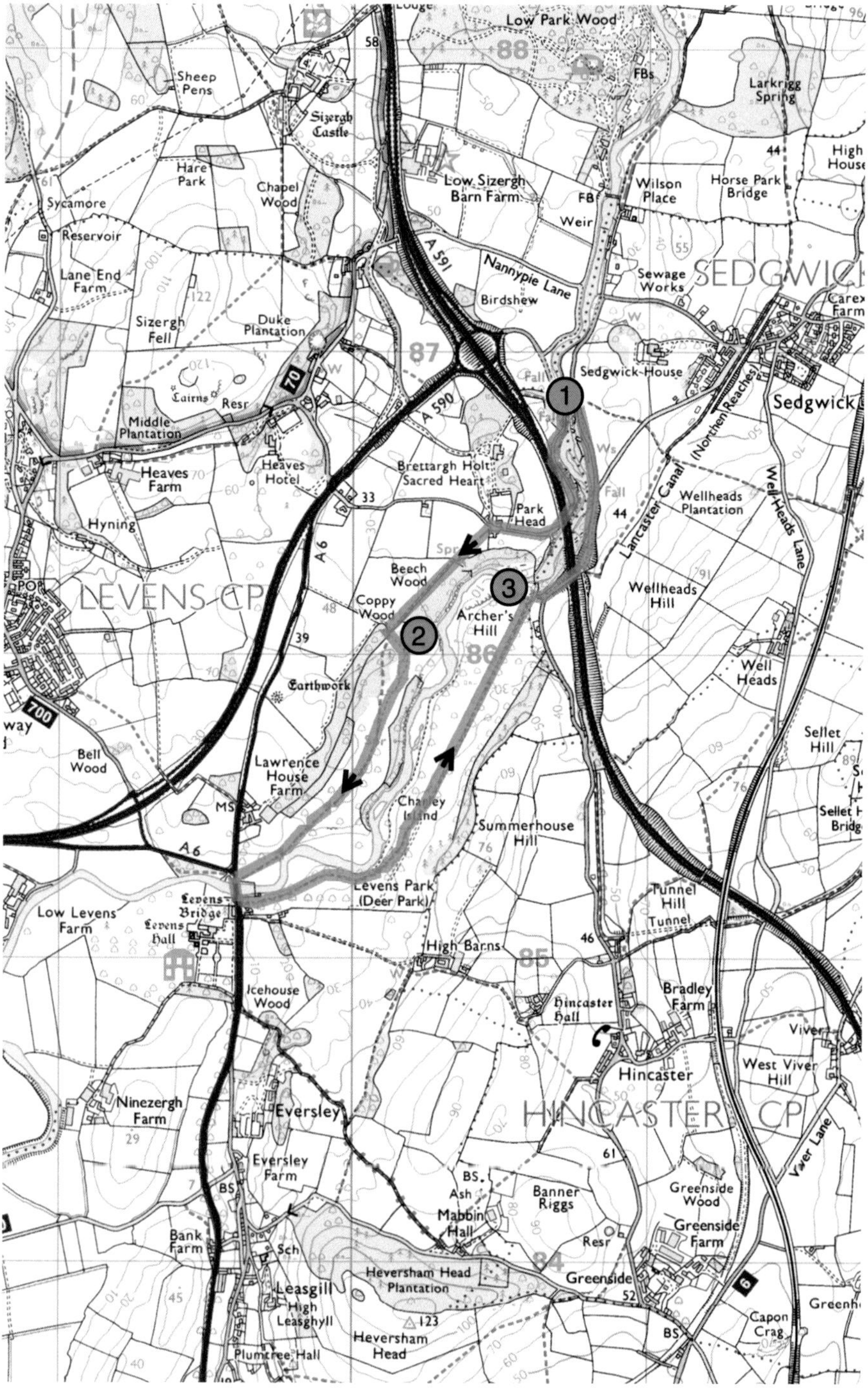
Low Park Wood
88
FBs
Larkrigg Spring
Sheep Pens
Sizergh Castle
Hare Park
Chapel Wood
Low Sizergh Barn Farm
Wilson Place
Horse Park Bridge
High House
Sycamore
Reservoir
FB
Weir
A 591
Nannypie Lane
Lane End Farm
Sewage Works
SEDGWICK
Carex Farm
Sizergh Fell
Duke Plantation
Birdshew
87
70
Cairns
Resr
Middle Plantation
Sedgwick House
Sedgwick
A 590
Fall
1
Heaves Farm
Heaves Hotel
Brettargh Holt Sacred Heart
Hyning
33
Park Head
44
Lancaster Canal (Northern Reaches)
Wellheads Plantation
Well Heads Lane
A6
Beech Wood
3
LEVENS CP
Coppy Wood
Archer's Hill
Wellheads Hill
2
39
86
Earthwork
Well Heads
700
Bell Wood
Lawrence House Farm
Sellet Hill
Chaney Island
Summerhouse Hill
Sellet Hill Bridge
MS
A6
Levens Park (Deer Park)
Tunnel Hill
Tunnel
Low Levens Farm
Levens Bridge
Levens Hall
High Barns
85
46
Icehouse Wood
Hincaster Hall
Bradley Farm
Viver
West Viver Hill
Hincaster
Ninezergh Farm
Eversley
HINCASTER CP
Viver Lane
Eversley Farm
61
BS
Ash
Banner Riggs
Greenside Wood
Mabbin Hall
Greenside Farm
Bank Farm
Sch
Resr
84
Heversham Head Plantation
Greenside
52
Leasgill
High Leasghyll
123
Capon Crag
Heversham Head
Plumtree Hall
BS

1 Set out in a southerly direction from the layby along the lane on the west side of the Kent, and continue past some cottages on the left until you reach the A590 dual carriageway bridge across the river. Follow the concrete right of way under the dual carriageway and up steps onto the paved country lane on the other side, heading towards the hamlet of Park Head.

Beyond the buildings to the left, take the signposted path over a wall stile and head diagonally left over the field to another wall stile at the bottom of a small incline. Continue uphill along the edge of the next field, staying close to the wall on the left which bounds Beech Wood. At the top of the field cross the wall stile on the left, taking you into Levens Park.

2 Follow the grassy path downhill through the park, bearing right and continuing down and alongside the Kent, to the stile onto the Milnthorpe road at Levens Bridge. Across the road you will see the entrance to Levens Hall. Turn left to cross the bridge on the pavement and left again through the stile at the other side which leads you down some steps onto the east side of the park. Continue uphill along the clear path which allows pleasant views of the Kent and the occasional sighting of deer and goats. The path eventually levels out and heads along 'Oak Avenue'.

3 At the northern end of the park, next to the park signage, take a further stile on the right, onto the road into Sedgwick. Go left on this road, crossing the dual carriageway and continue on, taking the left-hand fork to arrive back at the bridge over the Kent after about 800 metres.

GOATS ON OAK AVENUE
(Roger Blamire)

Trail S5: Cartmel

This trail starts at the Racecourse car park on the west side of the village of Cartmel, a short distance from the village centre. It takes in parts of the 185 mile Cumbria Coastal Way between Silverdale in Lancashire and Gretna, across the Scottish Border in Dumfries and Galloway, and the Cistercian Way, a route of 25 miles from Morecambe Bay to Roa Island peninsula at the southernmost point of the Furness Peninsula.

The trail covers some National Trust land, woods and fields. Cartmel Priory was originally founded in 1190 and parts of the existing building date from the 15th century.

Approximate Distance:	7.0 km/4.5 miles.
Terrain:	Paths and road.
Severity:	Relatively level terrain throughout.
Approximate Time:	35-50 minutes.
Total Ascent:	149m.
Start of the Trail:	From Plumgarth Roundabout to the north of Kendal, travel south on the A590 dual carriageway towards the M6, bypassing Kendal, and exit at the roundabout and sign for Barrow. Head west towards Barrow for approximately 6 miles and, after passing the roundabout and signage for Grange, come off the main road at the sign for Cartmel on the left-hand side of the road, just before Low Newton. Continue following the signage for Cartmel for a further three miles. Head towards the centre of the village, passing the Priory on the way, and you will reach the racecourse car park through the narrow lane to the left of the old post office at the far end of the main square. The pay car park is inside the southern boundary of the racecourse.
Map Reference:	SD 376 788 (OS Explorer Map OL7: South-Eastern Lakes – South Sheet)

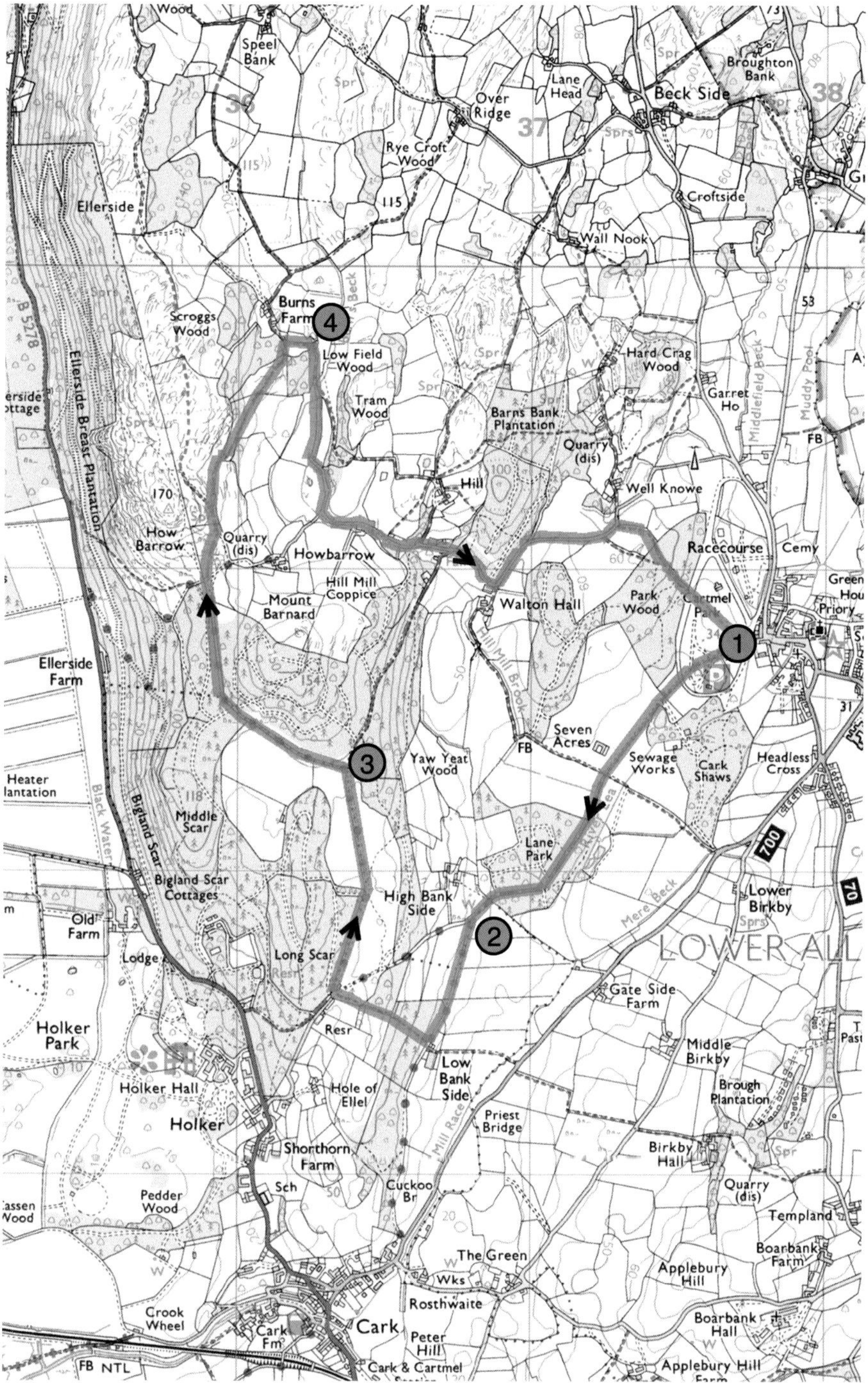

Speel Bank
Over Ridge
Lane Head
Beck Side
Broughton Bank
Rye Croft Wood
Elleriside
Croftside
Wall Nook
Burns Farm
4
Scroggs Wood
Low Field Wood
Tram Wood
Hard Crag Wood
Garret Ho
Middlefield Beck
Muddy Pool
Ellerside Breast Plantation
Barns Bank Plantation
Quarry (dis)
Hill
Well Knowe
How Barrow
Quarry (dis)
Howbarrow
Racecourse
Cemy
Hill Mill Coppice
Mount Barnard
Walton Hall
Park Wood
Cartmel Park
Priory
1
Ellerside Farm
Hill Mill Brook
Seven Acres
Sewage Works
Cark Shaws
Headless Cross
3
Yaw Yeat Wood
Heater Plantation
Middle Scar
Black Water
Bigland Scar
Lane Park
Bigland Scar Cottages
High Bank Side
Lower Birkby
Old Farm
Mere Beck
2
LOWER ALL
Lodge
Long Scar
Gate Side Farm
Holker Park
Resr
Low Bank Side
Middle Birkby
Holker Hall
Hole of Ellel
Brough Plantation
Holker
Priest Bridge
Mill Race
Shorthorn Farm
Birkby Hall
Pedder Wood
Sch
Cuckoo Br
Quarry (dis)
Templand
The Green
Boarbank Farm
Wks
Applebury Hill
Crook Wheel
Rosthwaite
Cark
Cark Fm
Peter Hill
Boarbank Hall
FB
NTL
Cark & Cartmel
Applebury Hill

1 From the car park follow the sign for the bridleway on the Cistercian Way, heading south west along the wide path across the southern end of the racecourse. Continue on through Lane Park Wood, and up a short incline at the end of the trees until you come to a junction with a paved lane on the left.

2 Go down the lane until you reach the white rendered building at Low Bank Side on the left-hand side. Look for the tall pedestrian gate on the other side of the lane and pass through, wending your way uphill on the narrow path through the former plantation, to reach the corner of a wood. Cross the stile and head through the wood on the clear path until you reach a wall stile on the far side.

Continue the short distance over a field to a junction of paths at Long Scar. Take the second path to the right, rejoining the Cistercian Way, and head slightly uphill, adjacent to the boundary wall of Long Scar woods on the left. Once clear of the woods continue on to the junction with the Cumbria Coastal Way.

3 Turn left through a gate onto the Way and follow the walled track as it bends to the right for 800 metres, until you reach a further gate. At this point, cross the field on the loosely defined path heading right, to a gate in the field wall. Turn left just before the gate and follow the path with the wall on your right, ignoring the farm track which heads off to the left. You will soon come to a gate in the wall, with signage, which directs you on a clear path over a field to a further gate into a caravan park, just before Burns Farm.

4 Follow the paved lane through the caravan park, as it heads sharply to the right and bends sharp right again. Continue on the lane for approximately 1,500 metres, ignoring the offshoots to the right and left, heading downhill and looping past Walton Hall Farm on the right. Look for the footpath sign on the right-hand side of the road just as the lane takes a sharp left towards Well Knowe.

Follow the distinct path through the field and into Park Wood, heading steeply downhill to emerge at the racecourse. You will see the car park on the other side which is accessible by right of way across the course. During race days and other events such as concerts you may have to take a detour round the course but there will be clear alternative signage to assist you.

THE START OF THE TRAIL FROM CARTMEL RACE COURSE
(Lois Blamire)

Trail S6: Helsington Church and Sizergh Castle

This trail starts at Helsington St John's Church which was built in 1726 from an endowment by John Jackson of nearby Holeslack Farm. The isolated position of the church owes much to proximity of the farm.

The trail passes next to Sizergh Castle, which is a stately home and garden, about four miles south of Kendal. The castle, a Grade I listed building, is in the care of the National Trust along with its garden and estate. It is the home of the Hornyold-Strickland family. The trail continues on fields and country roads past Levens village and over meadow back to the church.

Approximate Distance:	6.0 km/3.75 miles.
Terrain:	Paths, grass and road, with a relatively large number of gates to negotiate.
Severity:	Relatively easy with the exception of two long uphill sections over fields.
Approximate Time:	30-45 minutes.
Total Ascent:	136m.
Start of the Trail:	Take the signposted road west out of Kendal towards the village of Brigsteer. About quarter of a mile before the village the road takes a sharp right downhill. At this bend take the farm track to the immediate left and drive for approximately 200 yards to the parking area adjacent to Helsington Church.
Map Reference:	SD 489 890 (OS Explorer Map OL7: South-Eastern Lakes – South Sheet).

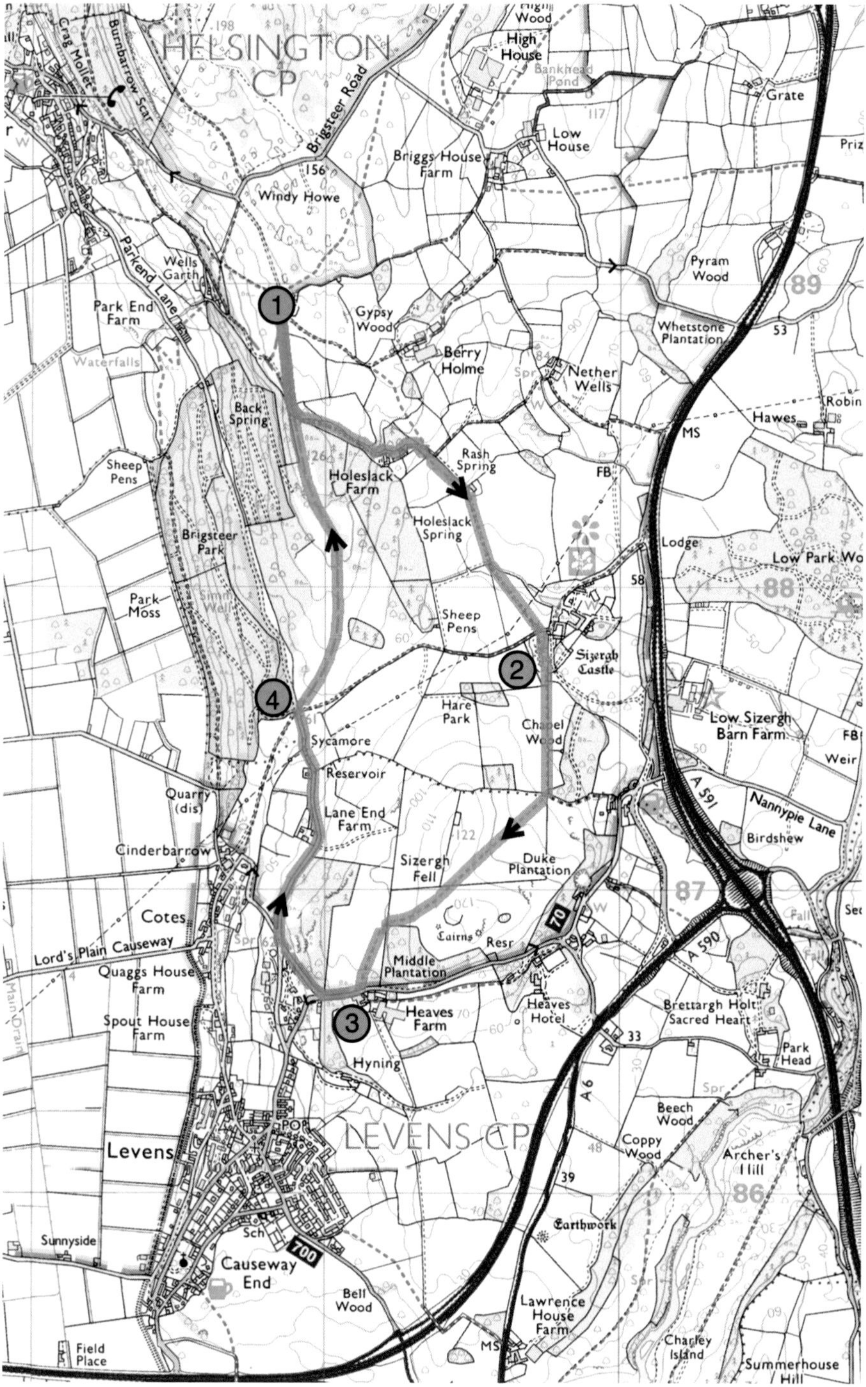
HELSINGTON CP
Brigsteer Road
Windy Howe
High Wood
High House
Bankhead Pond
Grate
Low House
Briggs House Farm
Pyram Wood
Wells Garth
Parkend Lane
Park End Farm
Gypsy Wood
Berry Holme
Nether Wells
Whetstone Plantation
Back Spring
Holeslack Farm
Rash Spring
Hawes
Sheep Pens
Brigsteer Park
Holeslack Spring
Lodge
Low Park Wo
Park Moss
Sheep Pens
Sizergh Castle
Hare Park
Chapel Wood
Low Sizergh Barn Farm
Sycamore
Reservoir
Quarry (dis)
Lane End Farm
Nannypie Lane
Birdshew
Cinderbarrow
Sizergh Fell
Duke Plantation
Cotes
Lord's Plain Causeway
Cairns
Resr
Middle Plantation
Quaggs House Farm
Heaves Farm
Heaves Hotel
Brettargh Holt Sacred Heart
Spout House Farm
Hyning
Park Head
Beech Wood
LEVENS CP
Levens
Coppy Wood
Archer's Hill
Earthwork
Sunnyside
Sch
Causeway End
Bell Wood
Lawrence House Farm
Field Place
Charley Island
Summerhouse Hill
A 591
A 590
A 6
1
2
3
4

1 Set out in a southerly direction from the church. At the end of the straight, take the left-hand fork and pass through a field gate, following the steep concrete track down the hill to Holeslack Farm. Pass through the gate at the bottom of the hill and follow the waymark signage bearing you to the left[12]. Follow the farm track for a short distance and pass through the pedestrian gate on the right, taking you into woodland. Go down the steps and follow the clear path downhill to a gate at the end of the woods. Turn right, through the gate, and cross two fields on the direct path, to reach the cafeteria and car park at Sizergh Castle.

2 Go through the pedestrian gates straight ahead and run past the café terrace, heading for another pedestrian gate at the far left-hand end of the car park. Negotiate the gate and follow the straight path along the edge of the field, with a wall on the left. At the end of the field pass through another pedestrian gate and follow the path which leads you diagonally right and uphill for 500 metres to another gate. Take the path to the right which heads downhill to another pedestrian gate in the field wall. Bear left and carry on downhill to the field boundary.

3 Pass through a timber gate opposite Heaves Farm, and turn right onto the road, heading towards Levens. After a short distance take the first right-hand fork in the road towards the hamlet of Cotes and then another right fork which leads you past Lane End Farm to the edge of the woods at Brigsteer Park, on the left.

4 Leave the road at this point, going over a wall stile on the right-hand side, and immediately through the gate to the left which leads you uphill over a grassy meadow. Follow the waymarks bearing you right at the top of the hill on a steeper incline past an isolated field stone. Pass through a wide gap in the trees, head sharp left at the waymark and follow the grassy path to another gate. Pass through and go slightly uphill over stony ground and across the next field, until you reach another gate onto the path from Helsington Church, which leads you back to the start of the run.

HELSINGTON ST JOHN'S CHURCH AT THE START OF THE TRAIL
(© Jumpy James)
www.jumpyjames.co.uk

[12] There is alternative at this point, taking you down to the right to a waymark, across the former farm orchard and into woodland. A clear path through the woods takes you to a pedestrian gate onto pasture. Bear left across the field to reach a gate and enclosed track which leads you to the castle car park at 2.

Trail S7: Grange-over-Sands and Hampsfell

Grange-over–Sands, on the north side of the huge expanse of Morecambe Bay, developed in the Victorian era from a small fishing village, and the arrival of the railway in 1857 made it a popular seaside resort.

The trail passes through Eggerslack Wood which is currently being coppiced over a ten-year programme to encourage regeneration. Temporary deer fences have been erected to facilitate this exercise. The moorland on Hampsfieldis very popular with walkers and visitors to the 'Hampsfield Hospice', a limestone tower monument (built in 1846), at the summit. The run affords panoramic views in every direction, including Morecambe Bay, the estuaries of the Leven and the Kent, and the distant fells of Central Lakeland.

Grange is on the Furness Railway Line which runs between Lancaster and Barrow and there are regular buses from Kendal (taking 40 minutes) and other nearby towns.

Approximate Distance:	7.5 km/4.75 miles.
Terrain:	A combination of rocky and grassy footpaths, and short sections of paved country lane.
Severity:	Deceptively tough with long sections of steep uphill and downhill, and pleasant running on generally level paths in between.
Approximate Time:	45-60 minutes.
Total Ascent:	370m.
Start of the Trail:	From Plumgarth Roundabout head south on the A591 dual carriageway, bypassing Kendal. Come off at the signage for Barrow and travel west on the A590. In approximately 6 miles, after passing the promontory of Whitbarrow Scar on the right, come off at the roundabout and onto the B5277 signposted for Grange. Pass through Lindale and enter Grange, passing the railway station on the left to reach a roundabout. Take the B5271 Windermere Road to the right from here and almost immediately park at the pay car park on the right-hand side of the road.
Map Reference:	SD 412 782 (OS Explorer Map OL7: South-Eastern Lakes – South Sheet)

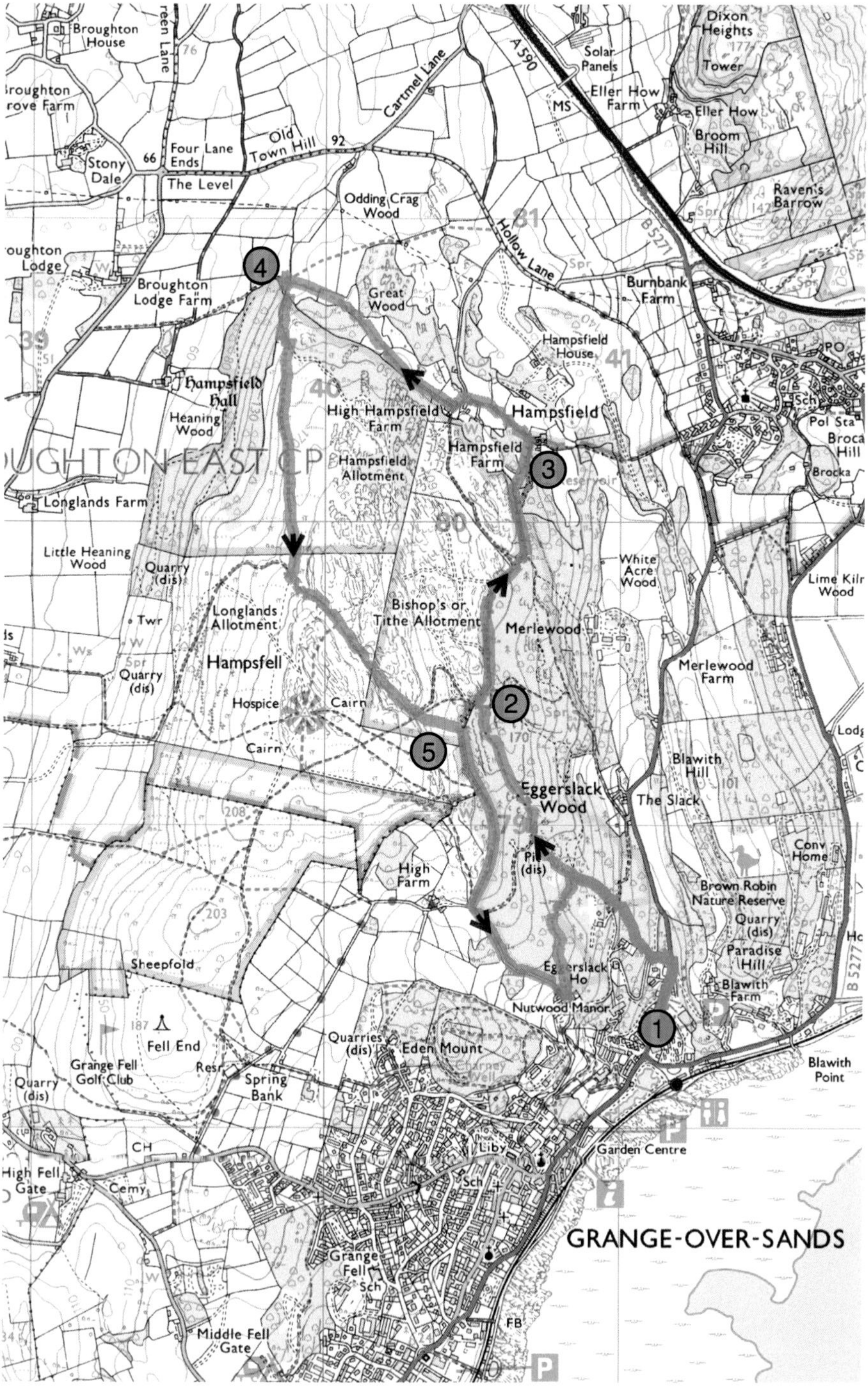
Broughton House
Four Lane Ends
The Level
Stony Dale
Old Town Hill
Cartmel Lane
A 590
Solar Panels
Eller How Farm
Dixon Heights
Tower
Eller How
Broom Hill
Raven's Barrow
Odding Crag Wood
Hollow Lane
Burnbank Farm
Broughton Lodge Farm
Great Wood
Hampsfield House
Hampsfield Hall
Heaning Wood
High Hampsfield Farm
Hampsfield
Hampsfield Farm
Hampsfield Allotment
Longlands Farm
Little Heaning Wood
Quarry (dis)
White Acre Wood
Longlands Allotment
Bishop's or Tithe Allotment
Merlewood
Hampsfell
Hospice
Cairn
Merlewood Farm
Blawith Hill
The Slack
Eggerslack Wood
High Farm
Conv Home
Brown Robin Nature Reserve
Paradise Hill
Blawith Farm
Eggerslack Ho
Nutwood Manor
Sheepfold
Fell End
Grange Fell Golf Club
Quarries (dis)
Eden Mount
Spring Bank
Blawith Point
Garden Centre
Liby
High Fell Gate
Cemy
Grange Fell
Sch
Middle Fell Gate
GRANGE-OVER-SANDS
B 5277
B 5271
1
2
3
4
5

1 Set out to the north on Windermere Road and in a short distance look for the footpath sign for Routen Well and Hampsfield on the left. Pass through the wall gap and onto a rocky path heading uphill through Eggerslack Wood. Cross the paved private lane to Eggerslack House and look for the footpath sign for Hampsfell. Follow the waymarks at the next paved private lane (to Eggerslack Cottages) in the direction of the large footpath sign guiding you left then right through the woods.

The path becomes less rocky as you pass an offshoot to the right, continuing on the main path straight ahead, and following the waymarks and a large sign for 'Public Footpath Hampsfield'. The path passes a disused concrete pit on the right and, after a further few metres of running, begins to level out. Carry on to the boundary wall at the western edge of the woods. Go over the stone stile and out of the woods to reach a four-way footpath sign.

2 Go right on the Restricted Byway signed for Hampsfield with the wall on your right, and along a grassy and muddy path. Pass a ladder stile at a gate with a footpath sign left to High Hampsfield. Ignore the sign and continue straight on, following the wall as it bends to the left, to reach a gate and adjacent wall gap into woodland. At the waymark on the other side of the wall take the left fork continuing on the Restricted Byway to reach a gate into a field at the edge of the woods. Follow the grassy path bearing slightly to the right across the meadow to a distant waymark. Pass through a gate onto an enclosed path to reach a paved lane at Home Farm and a three-way sign on the left.

3 Head left on the Restricted Byway along the lane to reach a Public Bridleway sign at High Hampsfield Farm. Turn left into the farm, following the bridleway sign to 'Grange over Sands 1¾ miles'. Go right before the farmhouse to follow a waymark guiding you between farm buildings and onto a muddy path with a wall on the right and woods on the left. At the end of the path go through the gate into a field and head downhill across the grass, passing an old lime kiln, to reach a wall stile and waymark at the bottom of the hill, where you will see the Central Fells in the distance. Continue to another stile and down to a solitary tree on the edge of woods.

4 Ignore the waymark guiding you to the right and take a sharp left and up to a gate and waymark into 'Hampsfield Allotment'. The path heads to the right and uphill to reach a plateau with panoramic views of green fields in the valley, the distant fells, and the estuary of the River Leven at Cartmel Sands. After passing through a wooden kissing gate, take the left hand fork up a grassy path to a waymark sign at a rocky promontory. Carry on to another waymark at the high point of the run to enjoy the views in all directions, including Morecambe Bay to the south and the Kent Estuary and Arnside to the east. Continue on downhill to a gate with another waymark sign. The path eventually bears left and down the steep hill, back towards Eggerslack Wood.

5 At the boundary wall, next to an obscured waymark, turn right and downhill to a metal gate and ladder stile. Cross the stile and continue on the path next to the wall on the left, and a fence on the right, and through a gate into woods. Shortly you will descend to reach the farm track to High Farm.

Go left at this point and downhill as the track merges into a paved lane. As you enter the outskirts of Grange, look for the large sign on the left for 'Public Footpath to Windermere Road'. Go through the wall gap into the woods and follow the path uphill before looping round to the right to take a steep downhill back to the outgoing path. Carry on down, across the two paved lanes, to Windermere Road, turn right and retrace your steps to the car park.

LOOKING BACK FROM THE MUDDY TRACK TO HIGH HAMPSFIELD FARM
(The Author)

BIBLIOGRAPHY

BOOKS

Richard Askwith, *'Feet in the Clouds'*
Aurum Press Limited, 2004

Steve Chilton, *'It's a Hill, Get Over It'*
Sandstone Press, 2014

Steve Chilton, *'Running Hard: The Story of a Rivalry'*
Sandstone Press, 2017

Steve Chilton, *'All or Nothing At All: The Life of Billy Bland'*
Sandstone Press, 2020

Alfred Wainwright, *'A Pictorial Guide to the Lakeland Fells: Book Two - The Far Eastern Fells'*
Westmorland Gazette, 1957

Alfred Wainwright, *'A Pictorial Guide to the Lakeland Fells: Book Seven - The Western Fells'*
Westmorland Gazette, 1966

INTERNET

Wikipedia

MAPS

OS Explorer Map OL2: Yorkshire Dales: Southern and Western Areas

OS Explorer Map OL6: The English Lakes: South-Western Area

OS Explorer Map OL7: The English Lakes: South-Eastern Area

OS Explorer Map OL19: Howgill Fells and Upper Eden Valley

ACKNOWLEDGEMENTS

Thanks to Joanna Mackenzie, Will Blamire, Ed Jones, and distance running greats Fergus Murray and Martin Hyman for their helpful comments on the text.

Lois Blamire and Roger Blamire provided splendid photographs and helped to convince me that my own feeble efforts were not worthy of the book. And particular thanks go to James Kirby whose professional touch undoubtedly was, and to Peter Todhunter who offered useful advice on copyright, and the Joss Naylor connection.

Leo Blamire provided vital assistance with maps and grateful thanks, too, go to Susan Edwards and Steven Findlay at Crawford Print and Design for their patience and skill in producing the finished article.

Finally, thanks to those long-suffering friends and relatives who endured my intensely preoccupied company on the reconnaissance trips round many of the trails.

INDEX OF PLACES

A

B

C

D

E

F

G

H

I

J

K

L

M

N

O

P

Q

R

S

T

U

V

W

X

Y

Z

INDEX OF PEOPLE AND ORGANISATIONS